CW01507580

animals of
Aotearoa

animals of Aotearoa

explore & discover New Zealand's wildlife

by Gillian Candler
illustrated by Ned Barraud

 potton & burton

Gillian Candler is an award-winning author who brings her knowledge and skills in education and publishing to her passion for the natural world. The more she learns about the extraordinary wildlife of Aotearoa, the more inspired she is to help protect our native species. When she's not writing books, she volunteers on conservation projects – counting birds, monitoring lizards, trapping pests and helping with bird and lizard translocations. She lives on the coast in Pukerua Bay.

Ned Barraud is an illustrator with a keen passion for the natural world. This passion was kindled early on, growing up tramping, camping and boating around Nelson and the Tasman Bay region. One of his enduring memories was being in a boat, surrounded by huge pilot whales that were so close, he could look into their eyes and see every scratch mark on their skin. Ned hopes this book will not only inspire kids to get out there and discover the creatures in this book but also protect them from threats facing them. He lives in Karori, Wellington, with his wife and three children.

other books in the explore & discover series

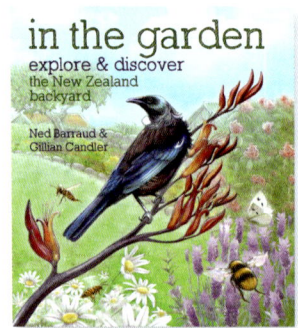
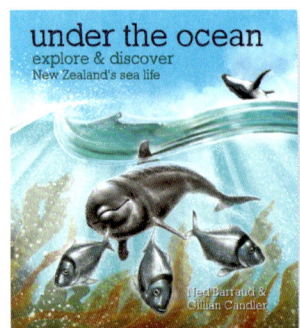

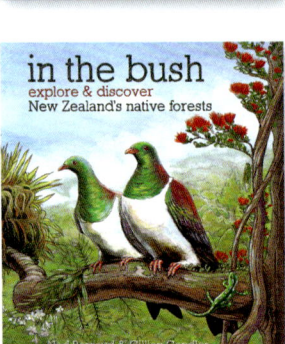
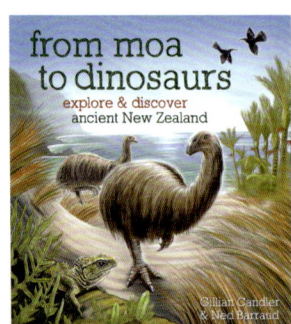
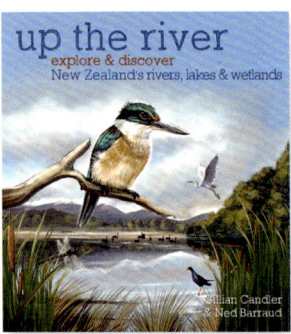

Many thanks to Don Newman and Andrew Stewart for advice during the writing of this book.

First published in 2018 by Potton & Burton
98 Vickerman Street, PO Box 5128, Nelson, New Zealand
www.pottonandburton.co.nz

Text © Gillian Candler; illustrations © Ned Barraud

ISBN 978 0 947503 89 5

Printed in China by Midas Printing International Ltd

This book is copyright. Apart from any fair dealing for the purposes of private study, research, criticism or review, as permitted under the Copyright Act, no part may be reproduced by any process without the permission of the publishers.

contents

introduction

We have many amazing and unique animals in Aotearoa New Zealand. Some aren't found anywhere else in the world, like the tuatara, which is the last surviving animal of its type, or the kākāpō, a nocturnal flightless parrot. One thing that might surprise you is that we have more than 10,000 kinds of native animals – though most of these are insects. That's lots more than we could include in this book!

In *Animals of Aotearoa* you can explore and discover many of our native animals – bats, birds, frogs and reptiles, as well as a wide range of insects, shellfish and fish. We've also included introduced animals that people have brought to New Zealand, such as blackbirds and deer.

But remember that this book is about animals that live *wild* in New Zealand; farm and zoo animals are not included.

Where do our animals come from?

HOW THE PAST AFFECTS WHICH ANIMALS LIVE IN AOTEAROA TODAY

Events in New Zealand's history have played a big part in determining which animals live here today. Around 80 million years ago, the land that would become New Zealand started to split from the great continent of Gondwana.

The ancient ancestors of some of New Zealand's wildlife are likely to have been on the land when Gondwana split up. These include freshwater insects and crayfish (kōura), tuatara, wētā, moa, wattlebirds such as kōkako, and native frogs.

Around 25 million years ago, much of what is New Zealand today was submerged under the ocean, with only a few small islands for animals to survive on. Later the land changed in shape and size, and at one stage the North and South islands were actually joined.

A male and the much larger female giant moa

ARRIVALS AND DEPARTURES

Fossils from around 19 million years ago, when New Zealand had a much warmer climate, show that crocodilians, land turtles and possibly small mammals lived here, but they wouldn't have survived the ice ages that occurred around 1-2 million years ago.

A freshwater crocodilian in a Central Otago lake, around 19 million years ago

However, New Zealand has been continually populated by new animals that find their way here. Some birds arrive by flying or being blown across from Australia in storms. Other animals could have arrived on 'rafts' of fallen trees and plants that were washed down rivers in other countries and carried here on ocean currents.

Recent bird arrivals from Australia include silvereye (tauhou) and spur-winged plover. Because all these animals arrived without human help, they are also called native animals.

ISLAND LIFE

Animals that have been here for millions of years have adapted to the conditions of life in New Zealand. Some have developed unique survival strategies, such as the kiwi, with nostrils at the end of its beak to smell out food.

Because there were no mammal predators, many birds became flightless as they no longer needed to fly away to escape being eaten.

Our native frogs survived by 'freezing' when in danger because their main predators were birds that hunted by sight and movement. But introduced mammal predators that hunted by smell meant the freezing technique didn't work against them, which is why frogs are now endangered.

When animals evolve for a long time on isolated islands they can also become giants of their kind, for example, our giant wētā, one of the world's largest insects, or the kākāpō, the world's heaviest parrot.

Some animals survived on Aotearoa even though their relatives became extinct in other parts of the world. This happened with the tuatara.

Being surrounded by sea means that many animals haven't made it to New Zealand at all, which is why we have no crocodiles, snakes or scorpions, even though they live in Australia.

ANIMALS INTRODUCED BY PEOPLE

By the time people arrived in New Zealand, the land was home to birds, reptiles, insects and bugs, with the only land mammals being several species of bats.

People brought new species with them. First, Māori brought the kiore (Pacific rat) and kuri (dog). Then Europeans, who came on bigger ships, brought Norway rats, pigs, goats, cats and dogs. They brought rabbits, and when the rabbits over-ran farms, they brought in weasels, stoats and ferrets, which they hoped would keep rabbit numbers down. Other species that were imported include the brush-tail possum to create a fur industry.

New animals continue to be introduced by people, mostly by mistake, such as fruit flies, or when pets and farm animals escaped into the wild.

Both people and the animals they introduced have had an impact on our wildlife. Many birds, such as the moa, became extinct as a result of being hunted by people. Others couldn't survive the introduced rats and stoats, or the loss of their habitat, such as the huia and bush wren.

You can read more about New Zealand's past in our book *From Moa to Dinosaurs*.

The extinct bush wren

Where do our animals live?

HABITATS AND THEIR FEATURES

Before people arrived in Aotearoa, the most common habitats were **forests** (both on the lowlands and in the hills), **alpine** areas, **wetlands**, **rivers** and **lakes**, **beaches**, **estuaries** and **under the sea**. Each habitat has its own features – beaches have sand and rocks, forests have soil and rocks, estuaries have mud and sand, marine habitats have salty water, and lakes and rivers are freshwater.

CHANGES IN HABITATS

When Europeans arrived in the 1800s, many forest and wetland habitats began to disappear. Forests were cut down and wetlands were drained so people could create farms or build towns and cities. Unfortunately changes have also occurred as habitats have become polluted, such as rivers and lakes, which means some animals can't live in them anymore.

A HABITAT'S ECOSYSTEM

The animals and plants in a habitat are often dependent on each other for survival. Birds, insects, plants and fish need each other for food. They also depend on environmental conditions, such as how wet or dry, or warm or cold it is.

But animals also play their part in creating the environment – some animals are scavengers that clean up dead animals or rotting leaves, while plants filter out nutrients from the water to make a more suitable environment for animals to live in.

This relationship between animals and plants and the environment is called an **ecosystem**.

A wetland ecosystem

You can read more about particular habitats and ecosystems in our books *At the Beach*, *In the Garden*, *Under the Ocean*, *In the Bush*, and *Up the River*.

Conservationists have created sanctuaries with special fences to keep predators out, they've removed predators and pests from island sanctuaries, and many communities are now involved in trapping pests.

Animals under threat

SAVING OUR ANIMALS

Sadly, many native animals are now extinct. Others have only very small populations left and are being carefully managed to try and save them. Some of the best-known examples are the kākāpō, black robin and takahē, as well as lesser-known animals such as the Hamilton's frog.

There are many others that are declining in numbers. They need habitats to live safely in away from introduced predators, and many people around New Zealand are working hard to protect them.

Hamilton's frog

You can play your part in saving our native animals. Learning about them by reading this book is a good start. You can also:

- make sure your pets aren't endangering wildlife
- keep plastic and rubbish out of waterways and oceans
- make your garden a haven for birds and lizards

Animal names and groups

Scientists who study animals find it useful to group them with other animals that have similar **features**. For example, birds have feathers, mammals feed their young milk, and insects have six legs.

Animals in a group share a common ancestor, but some are more closely related than others. For example, kiwi are distantly related to other birds, but closely related to each other, they are in their own **family**.

Scientists believe that the kiwi's ancestors flew here around 50 million years ago before they lost their ability to fly.

Scientists use the word **species** to describe each different type of animal in a family. So, we have five different species of kiwi.

A useful word that describes animals that don't have backbones is **invertebrates**. Insects, spiders, snails, worms are all examples of invertebrates. The opposite word is **vertebrate**, animals that have backbones. The first groups in this book: birds, frogs (amphibians), reptiles, fish, mammals are all **vertebrates**.

Another way to describe groups of living things is by where they live, for example freshwater fish, or by their size (microscopic life).

MĀORI KNOWLEDGE

Māori described the natural world by the relationships between things. For example, te aitanga pepeke (the insect world) refers to the group of creatures that share the same features: four or more legs, sits in a crouching position, can leap or jump. This group includes butterflies and moths as well as spiders.

Māori traditions and myths also recognised relationships, for example, that tuatara and mangō (shark) were brothers, both being descended from the god of the sea, Tangaroa. Māori names for animals often describe an important feature; bird names can reflect the noise a bird makes, or its colour.

In this book, we use common names in English and Māori to describe animals. We know there is sometimes more than one common name in each language, but we haven't included them all.

In the Māori world, the tuatara (top) and the mangōpare (hammerhead shark, above) were brothers, both being descended from Tangaroa, the god of the sea.

Animals of Aotearoa is full of the many extraordinary wild animals we have in New Zealand. We hope it helps you identify animals that you have seen or have heard about, and maybe it will introduce you to others for the first time. But mostly we hope it encourages you to do your part to protect and preserve the animals that live in this beautiful land of Aotearoa.

kiwi

rowi Ōkārito brown kiwi

There are five different species of kiwi. This is an Ōkārito brown kiwi/
rowi, the most endangered species. There are less than 500 rowi. They
live in forests near Ōkārito in Westland as well as on a few predator-free
islands. For many years it was thought that kiwi were not in danger, but
dogs, pests, and loss of forests have made it hard for young kiwi to survive.
The Department of Conservation works with others to protect these birds.
Some eggs are taken from nests and hatched and raised in sanctuaries.
Once the rowi are strong enough to defend themselves against stoats, they
can be put back into the forest. 40 cm

Kiwi are the only bird with
nostrils at the end of their beak.
Having nostrils here makes it
easier to smell out food such
as worms.

tokoeka southern brown kiwi

Tokoeka means 'weka with a walking stick'. Have a look
at the weka on page 26 and perhaps you can see why
Māori gave tokoeka this name. Tokoeka live on Rakiura/
Stewart Island, in Fiordland and in Haast. Haast tokoeka are
as rare as rowi. There are thousands more of the Fiordland and
Rakiura tokoeka but they are still considered to be endangered. Kiwi are
nocturnal, hiding in burrows or hollow logs during the day and feeding
on worms and other invertebrates at night. Tokoeka on Rakiura are
unusual as they can sometimes be seen feeding during the day. 45 cm

kiwi pukupuku
little spotted kiwi

Little spotted kiwi are the smallest kiwi. They are extinct on the mainland and are only found in sanctuaries today. The largest population is on Kāpiti Island, north of Wellington. Kiwi lay one or two eggs. The eggs are huge compared to the mother kiwi's body – six times bigger than normal for a bird of their size. Not all kiwi look after their eggs and chicks in the same way. The little spotted kiwi father sits on the egg to incubate it. When the chick hatches it is able to find its own food but the father stays close by for a while. 30 cm

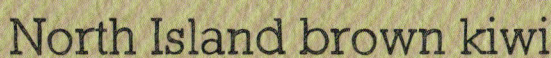

roa great spotted kiwi

The great spotted kiwi is found in the north-west of the South Island. Kiwi are flightless – they don't have tails and they don't even have wings they can flap like the flightless kākāpō. Their feathers are different from other birds too. Because they don't fly or swim, their feathers aren't smooth, instead they are fluffy and more like hair. The spotted pattern on the great spotted kiwi helps camouflage them in the bush. Kiwi feathers were used by Māori to make cloaks, which were usually for chiefs or other important people. 45 cm

North Island brown kiwi

This is the only kiwi found in the wild on the North Island. Kiwi make high-pitched whistles or shrieks. The male and female make different calls and can be heard replying to each other. Because kiwi are so hard to see at night, scientists count their calls to work out how many kiwi are around. The kiwi doesn't use its beak for fighting, it defends itself with its big claws. 40 cm

parrots

kākā

Kākā nest in holes in trees. They can live in towns and cities if there are plenty of trees and safe places to nest. They eat honeydew, fruit, nectar, tree sap and insects. Like the other parrots on this page, kākā can use their feet to hold food while they are eating. They can also use their beak like a claw to help them climb. 38–44 cm

kea

Kea are the only mountain parrot in the world. They live in mountains in the South Island. Their name comes from their call, which is a long 'keeeeaaa'. Scientists think that the kea is one of the most intelligent birds in the world. They are good at solving problems and very clever with their beak and claws. They are famous for their cheeky behaviour. They will steal food from tourists and quickly learn to open windows and doors. 46 cm

kākāpō

Kākāpō means 'night parrot'. One of the world's strangest parrots, they are nocturnal and flightless. But they can climb. They are also very big, and males can weigh up to 4 kilograms. Once a common bush bird, there are now only around 150. The Department of Conservation has a special programme to help the kākāpō. All the kākāpō are kept on predator-free islands. Eggs and chicks are carefully monitored to ensure they have the best chance of surviving. 58–64 cm

The most common of the kākāriki species, yellow-crowned kākāriki are forest birds. They also can be found on some sanctuary islands. They find food in the canopy, at the tops of trees, so are often heard rather than seen. Kākāriki eat seeds, fruit, flowers and invertebrates. Some people describe the noise they make as chattering or chuckling. 25 cm

kākāriki
yellow-crowned parakeet

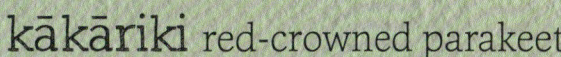

kākāriki red-crowned parakeet

The red-crowned kākāriki is rarer than the yellow-crowned kākāriki. One of the reasons for this is they often feed on the ground, eating seeds and fruit. This makes them vulnerable to predators. Kākāriki means 'small parrot' and is also Māori for the colour green. 25–28 cm

kākāriki
orange-fronted parakeet

Once thought to be extinct, there are very few of these kākāriki now. They are only found in a few places on the South Island and on a few predator-free islands. Some are being bred in captivity to be released back in to the wild. All kākāriki make their nests in holes in trees, which makes them easy prey to stoats and rats. To protect them, metal sheets are wrapped around trunks of trees where they are likely to nest. The metal prevents predators climbing up the trees. 20 cm

penguins

The three penguins on this page live around the mainland of New Zealand. Other penguins, such as rockhopper and Snares crested penguin, nest on offshore islands and are occasionally seen on mainland beaches.

hoiho yellow-eyed penguin

Hoiho means 'noise shouter'. They might be noisy but they are also shy and prefer to nest away from other penguins in forests, flax and on farmland. The world's rarest penguin, it lives only around the South Island and Stewart Island of New Zealand. 65 cm

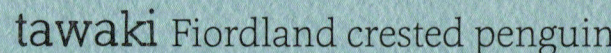

tawaki Fiordland crested penguin

Tawaki can be seen around Westland, Fiordland and Stewart Island. They often make their nests in forests or among rocks and in caves. Penguins sometimes have to swim a long way to find enough food. After their chicks have left the nest, the adult penguins go to sea to fatten up before they moult. Scientists have tracked these journeys and found they travel half way to Antarctica. All penguins use their wings like flippers to help them dive and swim. Their feathers keep them warm in the cold ocean. 40 cm

kororā little penguin

Also called little blue or blue penguins, they are the world's smallest penguins. They make nests in burrows or holes and will climb up to 300 metres to a nest site. Little penguins come ashore when it is dark, so you may have more chance of seeing one swimming in the sea during the daytime. All penguins need to moult to replace their feathers once a year. This takes about a month and they can't swim or feed until their new feathers grow back. Sometimes people living by the sea come across moulting kororā hiding in bushes. It is important to keep dogs away from them. 33 cm

herons

matuku moana
white-faced heron

White-faced herons are relative newcomers to
New Zealand. They can be seen by the sea, by rivers
and also in fields. They eat frogs, tadpoles, worms, fish,
mice and crabs. They stand very still so their prey can't
see them, then they dart very quickly to catch their prey
with their sharp beak. While they are mostly seen on the
ground, they roost and nest high up in trees. 67 cm

Kōtuku nest in only one place in New Zealand –
near Ōkārito in Westland. During the rest of the
year, they may fly to other wetlands and estuaries
around the country. In other countries, white
herons are called great egrets. Because the kōtuku
is seen only rarely, its feathers were
prized by Māori. 83–103 cm

kōtuku
white heron

matuku moana reef heron

The native reef heron is nationally endangered, there are
thought to be only 300–500 birds around New Zealand.
The reef heron is found on other Pacific Islands. Compared
to the white-faced heron, which usually keeps its neck
stretched out, they are quite squat and hunched.
They usually feed along the rocky shore
or in estuaries. 66 cm

seabirds

New Zealand has sometimes been called the seabird capital of the world. The birds on these two pages are just some of the many species that live in the oceans around New Zealand. Most nest on small islands where their chicks are safe from predators. All of these birds have tubenoses which they use to get rid of the salt from seawater. This means that they don't need to return to land to get fresh water.

toroa
Buller's mollymawk

Mollymawks are from the same family as the albatross. Like other albatrosses, the Buller's mollymawk feeds on fish and squid at the surface, rather than diving for food. wingspan up to 2 m

toroa ingoingo
royal albatross

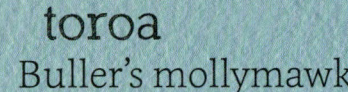

These huge birds have the longest wings of any bird. Rather than flap their wings, they glide on air currents. This is an efficient use of energy and makes it easier for them to spend months out at sea flying huge distances across the ocean. When they need to rest, they land on the sea. A colony of royal albatross can be seen at Taiaroa Head near Dunedin. wingspan up to 3.5 m

tāiko
Westland petrel

Children from Barrytown School, West Coast, discovered the Westland petrel in 1945, when doing a school project. Westland petrels are at risk from predators such as rats and stoats because they are one of the few seabirds that still nest on the mainland. length 48 cm

tītī sooty shearwater

Also called mutton birds, there are millions of sooty shearwaters. They breed in very large, closely packed colonies, mostly on small islands. Māori have traditionally collected tītī to eat and they continue to be an important food for some iwi. length 44 cm

New Zealand storm petrel

These little birds were thought to be extinct. But in 2003, birdwatchers on a ship in the Hauraki Gulf saw and photographed one. It took some detective work for scientists to find out where they were breeding, but eventually they found their burrows in the forest of Little Barrier Island. length 18 cm

pakahā fluttering shearwater

Named for their fluttering flight, these shearwaters are often seen in large flocks on the sea close to land. They dive underwater chasing small fish. Unfortunately, this means they can get caught in fishing nets. They nest in burrows on offshore islands. length 37 cm

titiwainui fairy prion

Fairy prions nest in burrows. On some small islands, these burrows can be taken over by tuatara, which will also eat any eggs or chicks that they find. Seabird colonies are smelly places. The bird's poo – guano – is a good source of fertiliser for the land, as well as a source of food for invertebrates. Fairy prions eat krill, small fish and squid. length 25 cm

tubenose
for removing
salt from water

19

river & shore birds

One of the most endangered gull species in the world, tarāpuka breed mostly on braided rivers (rivers that spread out into many winding channels that criss cross through stones and gravel. Most are in the South Island). The gulls' nests are at risk from cats, ferrets and stoats, vehicles driving on riverbeds and changes to river habitats. 35–38 cm

tarāpuka
black-billed gull

tarapirohe
black-fronted tern

Most terns live by the sea, but black-fronted terns nest and raise their young on braided rivers. They live in large, noisy groups. 28 cm

tara
white-fronted tern

Terns can pick small fish out of the water as they fly over the sea. They are usually seen in flocks and they nest in large colonies on cliffs or islands. 40 cm

tōrea oystercatcher

Oystercatchers use their long, orange beaks to reach down into the sand. Their beaks are strong enough to break open shells. They make their nests in the sand or among stones on the beach. 45 cm

karoro
black-backed gull

adult   juvenile

These gulls eat shellfish, such as mussels and tuatua. They are also scavengers and will eat your picnic food or dead fish that are washed up on the beach. Gulls nest on rocky cliffs. They can sometimes be seen dropping shellfish on to rocks to break open the shell. 60 cm

akiaki red-billed gull

Red-billed gulls are smaller than black-backed gulls. Their young have blackish beaks which turn red in their second year. They are social birds that like to live in groups. Although sea gulls seem quite common, scientists have found that there are fewer red-billed gulls than there used to be. 37 cm

poaka
pied stilt

kakī black stilt

Pied stilts are wading birds that like mudflats, harbours and rivers. Their long legs mean they can stand in water to look for shellfish, which they catch with their long beak. 35 cm

Kakī are one of New Zealand's rarest birds, and are now found only in braided rivers in a few South Island locations. Adult kakī are completely black, unlike the more common pied stilts, which are black and white. 40 cm

shore birds

kōtuku ngutupapa
royal spoonbill

Spoonbills flew here from Australia, and now nest and breed here. In the 1970s there were about 50 birds, now there are thousands. Spoonbills feed in estuaries, moving their bill back and forth in the water to filter out fish, shrimps and crustaceans. 80 cm

takapū gannet

Gannets can be seen flying above the sea spying for fish. Once they spot fish, they dive very fast – up to 145 kilometres an hour. Only about one third of their dives are successful. If they don't catch a fish first go, they might stay underwater to chase fish, hoping for a second chance. wingspan 1.8 m

tūturiwhatu
banded dotterel 20 cm

Dotterels eat insects and other invertebrates found among sand, mud and stones. Because they nest on the ground, dotterels survive best where there is predator control and protection from people, dogs and cars.

New Zealand dotterel 25 cm

22

kuaka godwit

Kuaka fly 12,000 kilometres non-stop from Alaska to New Zealand every spring. They spend our summer eating worms and shellfish on mudflats and beaches. In autumn they return to Alaska to breed. 40 cm

kawau pāteketeke spotted shag

Spotted shags dive from the surface and use their feet to help them swim underwater. Gannets and shags don't have nostrils, which makes it easier for them to dive. They breathe by opening their beaks when they are above the surface. height 70 cm

kawau paka little shag

Little shags are the smallest shags. They live around rivers and lakes as well as the shore. 56 cm

kāruhiruhi pied shag

Kāruhiruhi dive for fish, sometimes staying under water for 20 seconds. Once they are back on land, they hold their wings out to dry. Shags make nests in trees on the coast. 80 cm

23

wetland & river birds

kōtare sacred kingfisher

Kingfishers sit up high on rocks, trees or wires looking out for food. They eat fish, crabs, insects and other animals. Kingfishers have very good eyesight but can't move their eyes, so they move their head to watch their prey. 24 cm

pūkeko

Pūkeko mostly eat grass, rushes and sedges, which they hold with their feet and cut with their bills. Sometimes they eat insects, worms and young birds. 38–50 cm

spur-winged plover

Also called a masked lapwing, these noisy birds started arriving from Australia in the 1930s and are now living across much of New Zealand. They like open fields – farmlands and playing fields – as well as wetlands and beaches. 38 cm

female

male

warou
welcome swallow

If you see birds darting back and forth over the water's surface, they are likely to be welcome swallows catching insects. Swallows build nests out of mud, sometimes on the side of buildings or under eaves. 14–16 cm

pūtangitangi
paradise shelduck

These native ducks like living in fields as well as by water. Their population has increased as bush has been cleared to make fields. If you get close enough to pūtangitangi and listen carefully, you can hear that the male and female ducks make different noises. They mostly eat grass and other plants. 63 cm

ngutuparore
wrybill

Wrybills get their English name from their strange bills, which always curve to the right rather than downwards. This makes it easier for them to find insect larvae and snails under stones on the riverbed. 20 cm

pāpango
scaup

Australian coot

Scaup are diving ducks that are found mostly on lakes or large, slow rivers. Their legs are set back on their body, making it easier for them to swim but harder for them to walk on land. 40cm

The New Zealand coot is extinct, but the Australian coot can be found on lakes and ponds around the country. They make a floating nest of twigs and leaves that they attach to reeds or branches. 35–39 cm

wetland & lake birds

weka

Weka are cheeky birds. They'll snatch food from campers and raid the dog bowl outside a back door. They eat a wide variety of food, such as fruit, lizards, eggs and small birds. They might seem common, but their population is patchy, with few in the North Island. Weka can be seen on grasslands, beaches and forest edges as well as the wetlands. 50–60 cm

pūweto
spotless crake

Because spotless crakes live only in wetlands and are so secretive, no one knows how many there are. A similar bird is the marsh crake. They make their nests out of woven grass just above the water level. 20 cm

mātātā fernbird

Mātātā are rarely seen because they are poor flyers and prefer to stay hidden. They eat insects, spiders and other small creatures found in the wetlands. 18 cm

weweia
dabchick

Dabchicks are part of the grebe family. They live on shallow lakes and ponds around the North Island. Sometimes they're seen swimming with their chicks on their backs. 28–30 cm

pāteke brown teal

These unusual ducks are mostly nocturnal and often go searching for food a long way from water. Pāteke eat seeds, leaves and invertebrates. They like forest and wetlands, but as few lowland forests and wetlands exist, they have lost a lot of their habitat. They are now quite rare and survive mostly where there is some protection from predators. 48 cm

kāhu
swamp harrier

Kāhu are birds of prey, and often seen gliding and circling high in the sky. They hunt over swamps and fields, catching rabbits, mice and small birds. They also eat dead animals, for example, animals hit by cars. 50–60 cm

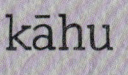

matuku hūrepo
Australasian bittern

When they are disturbed or feel threatened, bitterns freeze, their beaks pointing straight up in the air. Male bitterns make a booming sound during the breeding season. Bitterns eat fish, frogs, kōura and insects. 74 cm

pūteketeke
Australasian crested grebe

Pūteketeke are found on South Island lakes. They build floating nests out of sticks and waterweeds. 48–61 cm

forest birds

koekoeā
long-tailed cuckoo

Māori knew that the first songs of koekoeā and pīpīwharauroa were a sign that spring had arrived. Both cuckoos spend winter in the Pacific Islands and come to New Zealand to lay their eggs – in other birds' nests. They leave the other bird to feed their chick. Amazingly, the young bird knows where to fly off to in autumn. 40 cm

pīpīwharauroa
shining cuckoo

Cuckoos are well camouflaged and are more often heard than seen. The shining cuckoo lays its egg in a grey warbler nest. When the chick hatches it will kick out any grey warbler chicks or eggs so it gets all the food the parents bring. Adult shining cuckoos can eat caterpillars that are toxic for other birds. 16 cm

ruru morepork

Ruru catch insects, small birds, mice and other prey at night. Ruru are also found in Australia, where they are called boobook owls. Try saying all the different names – do they sound like the bird's call? 29 cm

28

kererū/kūkupa
New Zealand pigeon

Their big mouths mean kererū can swallow large seeds such as tawa and karaka. After eating the fruit, they poo out the seed. This helps new trees grow in different places in the forest. Kererū don't sing or call, they make a quiet cooing noise, but their wings make a lot of noise when they take off. 50 cm

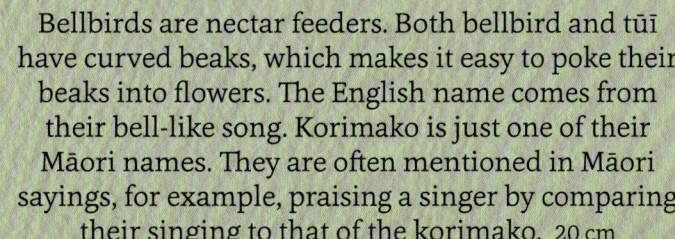

korimako
bellbird

Bellbirds are nectar feeders. Both bellbird and tūī have curved beaks, which makes it easy to poke their beaks into flowers. The English name comes from their bell-like song. Korimako is just one of their Māori names. They are often mentioned in Māori sayings, for example, praising a singer by comparing their singing to that of the korimako. 20 cm

tūī

Tūī eat nectar from flowering plants, such as flax. They also eat insects and fruit. When tūī eat nectar from flowers, pollen brushes off on their heads, which helps pollinate other flowers. Sometimes it looks like they are singing but no sound is coming out – it's because they can sing at a pitch that humans can't hear. 30 cm

forest birds

pīwakawaka
fantail

Fantails eat insects. They are friendly birds because they know people walking along will disturb insects, which they can then catch and eat. The pīwakawaka's tail helps it make quick movements in the air as it hunts flying insects. It builds several nests and lays more than one lot of eggs each year. 16 cm

riroriro grey warbler

Riroriro are insect eaters. Their grey feathers and tiny size mean they are often heard rather than seen. Their song is a long, beautiful trill. Sometimes a shining cuckoo will lay its egg in a grey warbler's nest and leave the warbler to raise the chick. 10 cm

kakaruia
Chatham Island black robin

The kakaruia was very close to extinction – in the 1970s there were only seven birds left on a remote island that is part of the Chatham Islands. A rescue effort involved using tomtits as foster parents and now there around 300 birds. The kakaruia is closely related to the South Island robin. There are also Chatham Islands species of tūī, warbler, tomtit and fantail, which are related to those in this book. 15 cm

male

female

miromiro tomtit

A tomtit guards its territory and is usually seen on its own or in a pair. There are slight differences in colour between South Island and North Island tomtits. 13 cm

toutouwai robin

The bird pictured here is a South Island robin. A North Island robin looks similar but with less white on its front. Robins will often come down onto forest tracks to eat insects that people disturb as they walk along. They can still be found in some forests, and with the help of pest trapping, there will be more places where you can see them. 18 cm

tauhou silvereye

Also called waxeyes or white-eyes, these little birds eat fruit and insects. They are often seen in flocks. Tauhou means 'stranger'. They arrived in New Zealand nearly 200 years ago having flown 2000 kilometres from Australia. As well as living in forests, they are also one of the most common garden birds. 12 cm

tītitipounamu rifleman

These are our smallest birds. Their Māori name has both the noise of its call – 'tītiti' and the colour of its feathers – 'pounamu'. Tītitipounamu eat invertebrates that they find in the bark of trees. 8 cm

forest birds

kōkako

Kōkako are only able to fly short distances – instead they glide and jump. Kōkako mainly eat fruit and leaves. Another name for the North Island kōkako is blue-wattled crow. South Island kōkako have orange wattles, with the last confirmed sighting of one in 2007. The North Island kōkako was rare, but numbers are slowly increasing as people try to protect them from predators. 38 cm

tīeke saddleback

By the middle of last century, North and South Island tīeke only survived on a couple of islands. In the 1960s, 36 tīeke were rescued from Big South Cape Island when it was overrun with rats. Today, there are more tīeke, but they can only be found in sanctuaries and on predator-free islands. Tīeke eat invertebrates that they find on the ground and under tree bark. 25 cm

hihi stitchbird

Hihi used to live in North Island forests but are now only in a few island and mainland sanctuaries. They nest in holes in trees. Hihi eat fruit, nectar and invertebrates. The bird pictured here is the male hihi. The female is greyish brown with some white on its wing. 20 cm

karearea New Zealand falcon

Falcons are raptors – they catch and eat live prey such as small birds. Unlike the swamp harrier that hovers in the air, falcons move swiftly, reaching speeds of over 100 kilometres per hour. Falcons live in forests but can also be found on farmland or in cities where there are plenty of trees. 40–50 cm

pīpipi brown creeper

Brown creepers are found only in the South Island and Rakiura/Stewart Island. They can be seen in noisy flocks in forests. Brown creeper, whitehead and mohua are all closely related. The long-tailed cuckoo likes to lay its egg in their nests, mostly using the brown creeper's nests in the South Island and the whitehead's nests in the North Island. 13 cm

mohua yellowhead

Mohua are found only in South Island and Rakiura/Stewart Island forests. They nest in holes in trees, which makes them vulnerable to predators as the parent sitting on the nest can't escape if attacked. For this reason, their numbers have declined and they are now only found in a few places. They do well in sanctuaries where there are no rats or stoats. 15 cm

pōpokatea whitehead

Found only in the North Island, whiteheads do best in sanctuaries such as Kāpiti Island and Little Barrier Island. They can still be found in other forests but their population is declining. They eat insects and spiders. 15 cm

mountain birds

The bird you are most likely to see and hear in the mountains of the South Island is the kea (page 14).

whio blue duck

Whio are unusual ducks. They live in clear, fast-flowing rivers surrounded by bush, but can also be found on mountain lakes. They have lost habitat through the clearing of land and building of dams. Their bills have soft edges that make it easier for them to feel insect larvae living underwater and under stones. They are mostly found only in mountainous areas today. 50–55 cm

takahē

Seventy years ago, people thought the takahē was extinct. Then in 1948, an expedition to the remote Murchison mountains in the South Island found takahē still alive. Since then scientists have worked hard to protect them and encourage them to breed. Some takahē have been moved to islands such as Tiritiri Matangi, and other sanctuaries. There are now around 350 takahē, so they are still very rare. Takahē are a distant relation to pūkeko, but takahē are heavier (2–3 kilograms compared to the pūkeko at 1 kilogram). Takahē are more colourful, they have stouter legs and much bigger beaks. 50 cm

pīhoihoi
New Zealand pipit

Pīhoihoi turn up in some surprising places.
They can be found in the mountains or by the
sea, as well as in fields and other open places.
They are often seen eating seeds or insects
on the ground. If you walk up to one, it will
usually run away rather than fly. 18 cm

pīwauwau rock wren

New Zealand once had several other species of wren.
Now only the rock wren and the rifleman are left.
These wrens all belong to an ancient family of tiny
birds. Rock wrens live in the mountains. They eat
insects and spiders that they find among the
alpine rocks. Although they can fly, they prefer
to hop around. They also nest on the ground,
which makes them vulnerable to stoats, and
their numbers are declining. 10 cm

introduced birds

female

male

blackbird manu pango

The female blackbird isn't black! Her brown colour makes it easier to hide in hedges and among the grass. Both parents feed the baby blackbirds. Sometimes you can see the young birds hopping along behind their parents waiting for food. 25 cm

chaffinch
pahirini

Chaffinches are members of the finch family. Other finches that are sometimes seen in gardens are greenfinches and goldfinches. Finches use their powerful beaks and gizzards for grinding up seeds. 15 cm

myna maina

Myna (or mynah) birds only live in the middle and north of the North Island. They are bossy and will attack other birds. They eat just about anything, including the eggs and chicks of other birds. 24 cm

song thrush

Song thrushes can be seen hopping around in the garden. Their favourite food is snails.
23 cm

female

male

sparrow pihoihoi

Sparrows are the most common garden birds in New Zealand. They were introduced to New Zealand because people thought they would help farmers by eating insect pests, but they eat more seeds than insects. Now many people think sparrows are pests. 14 cm

European goldfinch

These colourful little finches eat thistle seeds. Apart from when they are breeding, they can often be seen flying around together in flocks. 12 cm

starling
tāringi

Starlings eat insects, snails and spiders as well as fruit and nectar from plants. They nest in holes in trees or buildings. 21 cm

yellowhammer

Yellowhammers were brought to New Zealand from England 150 years ago. Yellowhammers eat grass seeds. 16 cm

introduced birds

California quail were introduced from the US as game birds (birds that people hunt and eat). The bird pictured here is the male. The female has fewer markings on her face and a smaller plume on her head. They have large families, with often more than 10 chicks. Although they are usually seen running along the ground, they are able to fly. 25 cm

California quail
kuera

The black swans we see today were introduced from Australia, but they are similar to a native swan that used to live in New Zealand. They mostly eat plants that grow underwater. Although swans can sometimes be seen on the sea, in harbours or estuaries, they can't live without fresh water. 110–140 cm

black swan kakīānau

common pheasant

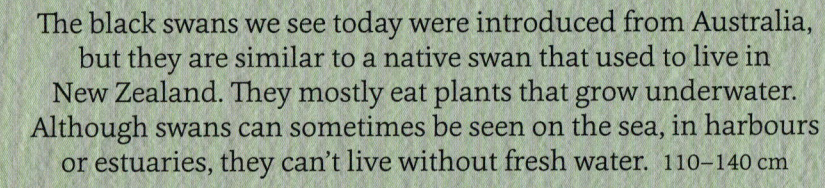

Pheasants like grasslands, farmlands and areas of scrub. The brightly coloured male has a distinctive long tail. The female is smaller, about 60 cm long, and is mostly brown with a shorter tail. Pheasants were introduced as game birds. 80 cm

Canada goose

People brought geese to New Zealand from Canada in the early 1900s to hunt. Geese are grass eaters so huge flocks can take over a field close to a lake or river, eating all the grass and leaving behind large amounts of goose poo. 85–95 cm

eastern rosella

Introduced here from Australia, eastern rosellas have been spreading through the North Island, and also can be found near Dunedin. They eat seeds, fruit and nectar. 30 cm

male

female

mallard duck rakiraki

Mallard ducks are an introduced species and are now the most common duck in New Zealand. Other birds that might look similar to female mallards are the grey duck, brown teal and the grey teal, all of which are native. All teal species are protected by law. up to 70 cm

Australian magpie

Magpies are aggressive birds and will attack other birds. During the breeding season when they have chicks to protect, they will sometimes dive-bomb and attack people. Magpies eat insects and other invertebrates. They were introduced to control insect pests, but they are now generally considered to be a pest themselves. 41 cm

native frogs

The Māori name for the native frog is pepeketua. Frogs are amphibians. Amphibians can breathe through their skin as well as their lungs. Their thin, delicate skin needs to be kept moist. Introduced frogs live in ponds and streams but our native frogs usually live in moist places under logs or stones. Their tadpole stage is completed in the egg, so little froglets hatch from the eggs. Native frogs don't have eardrums, and they don't croak.

Hochstetter's frog

This is the only native frog that lives near water. It is the most widespread, found in various places on the North Island and also Great Barrier Island. Hochstetter's frogs leave their young froglets to look after themselves. up to 4.8 cm

Archey's frog

The father Archey's frog carries his little froglets on his back until they are ready to live independently. These forest-dwelling frogs like damp places but don't live in streams. They are only found now in three places on the North Island. up to 3.7 cm

Hamilton's frog

This is one of the rarest frogs in the world with less than 300 animals. They are all found on Stephen's Island. up to 5 cm

Maud Island frog

These nocturnal frogs like being out and about on misty evenings, but they don't go far, often staying within a few metres of one spot for years. They are found on Maud Island, and some have been moved to Motuara Island. up to 5 cm

introduced frogs

green & gold bell frog

Originally from Australia, these frogs now live in the upper half of the North Island. They lay their eggs in shallow ponds. After a few days tadpoles hatch out and swim around. It takes a couple of months for the tadpoles to change: they grow legs and lose their tails. Eventually they turn into adult frogs that can leave the water. up to 9 cm

southern bell frog

These Australian frogs are now the most common frog found in New Zealand. They prefer lakes and swamps to shallow ponds. If you hear a frog croaking, you know it's an introduced frog because native frogs don't croak. up to 10 cm

brown tree frog

Also from Australia, brown tree frogs are found in the South Island and parts of the North Island. They are a similar size to native frogs but unlike native frogs they have an eardrum, which is easy to see. up to 4 cm

eardrum

reptiles

New Zealand's reptiles are tuatara, lizards (mokomoko) and turtles. New Zealand has over 100 species of lizards, which are either geckos or skinks. A few species of turtles are found in the ocean around New Zealand. Reptiles and amphibians are ectotherms – they have to warm themselves up in the sun or from another heat source. This is why they are often seen basking in the sun during the daytime.

crest

tuatara

In Māori, tuatara means 'spiny back'. Tuatara eat beetles, wētā and other small creatures. Scientists once called tuatara 'living fossils' but they now know that tuatara are not identical to their ancient ancestors, although they are the only surviving species in the *Rhynchocephalian* order of reptiles. up to 60 cm long

New Zealand has around 40 species of gecko, but many are rare, such as the Duvaucel's gecko. It is one of the world's largest geckos. These huge geckos survive on offshore sanctuary islands. They are thought to live to 30–50 years old. They eat insects, plant nectar, small lizards or birds' eggs. up to 16 cm long, not including tail

Duvaucel's gecko

raukawa gecko

Raukawa geckos are common around the Cook Strait region. They are nocturnal and can sometimes be found living in sheds or houses. All lizards shed their skins when they get too tight – a new skin is growing underneath. Sometimes you can find a complete empty skin that a gecko has left behind. Geckos are great climbers, their special feet can 'stick' to surfaces. This means they can even walk upside down on your ceiling or on a pane of glass. up to 8 cm long, not including tail

forest gecko

Forest geckos live in trees. There are at least two different species – the forest gecko and the ngahere gecko. They eat insects as well as berries and nectar. Each gecko has a different pattern on its back, so scientists can take photos of the pattern to identify them. Geckos don't have eyelids, so they can't keep their eyes moist by blinking. Instead they lick their eyes with their tongue. up to 9 cm long, not including tail

green gecko

Different species of green gecko are found in different parts of New Zealand. They are hard to see because they are so well camouflaged. Green geckos are usually active during the day. All lizards are protected and can't be kept as pets unless you have a permit. Unfortunately, some people collect geckos and try to smuggle them out of New Zealand. up to 9.5 cm long, not including tail

43

Otago skink

Otago skinks are a larger skink species. They are very rare and now only live in a small part of Otago. They are thought to live up to 20 years. up to 12.5 cm long, not including tail

ornate skink

Ornate skinks like moist places and are most active at dawn and dusk. Like most of New Zealand's geckos and skinks, the ornate skink gives birth to live young. This is unusual as most lizards in other countries lay eggs. up to 8 cm, not including tail

common skink

If you see skinks darting across a coastal or grassy pathway on a sunny day, they may well be common skinks, sometimes called grass skinks. There are at least six different species of common skink. They hunt insects during the daytime. All skinks have smooth, glossy skins, unlike geckos, which have rougher, baggy skins. up to 8 cm, not including tail

copper skink

Our smallest skink, the copper skink is fairly common in the North Island. It is nocturnal. All skinks and geckos can drop their tail when in danger, the tail will regrow, although it may look different from the rest of the skink. Scientists usually measure lizards and gecko from head to base of tail for this reason. up to 6 cm, not including tail

plague or rainbow skink

An Australian intruder, plague skinks are unwanted in New Zealand. They quickly take over the habitat of native skinks and compete with them for food. They are found in parts of the North Island. They are smaller than native skinks, and unlike native skinks, they lay eggs. 5.5 cm, not including tail

leatherback turtle honu

These turtles like feeding in the cooler water around New Zealand but they return to Australia and the Solomon Islands to breed and lay their eggs. Other turtles such as green turtles are sometimes found around the north of the North Island. Turtles need to breathe air so they must come up to the surface to breathe. Unfortunately, turtles are at risk from rubbish in the sea – they sometimes eat plastic bags because they look like jellyfish, and they can also get entangled in lines or ropes. up to 2 m

native freshwater fish

banded kōkopu

Banded kōkopu eat insects and spiders that fall into the water, as well as some of the animals that live in creeks and rivers. They and other kōkopu as well as kōaro and mudfish are members of the galaxiid family. They got their name because some galaxiids have spots, which made people think of a galaxy of stars. up to 30 cm

giant kōkopu

These large native fish live in deep dark places, in wetlands, lakes and coastal rivers. The population is declining, as there are fewer places for them to live. up to 58 cm

inanga

Inanga lay their eggs at high tide among grass in estuaries. Then on a following spring tide, the eggs hatch and the young are swept out to sea. After about six months at sea, the young fish that have survived return to the estuary and swim upstream. Adult inanga usually live for only a year. up to 19 cm

Whitebait are the young fish of inanga, kōaro, giant kōkopu, banded kōkopu and short-jawed kōkopu. The young of these fish swim out to sea once they have hatched, and when they are old enough, they swim back up estuaries and rivers. Many of these young fish get caught in nets and are eaten. No one knows how many of them are caught, but scientists think there are now fewer adult fish. People have also made changes to rivers and wetlands so there are fewer places for fish to lay their eggs.

kōaro

Kōaro can use their fins to climb up wet, natural rock barriers. They can't travel up rivers that have dams or concrete culverts, unless people also build 'fish ladders' for them to climb up. up to 18 cm

torrent fish

Torrent fish live in fast-flowing streams. They are well adapted to rushing water, their heads are streamlined and their large fins help them hold their place on the riverbed. up to 10 cm

waikaka brown mudfish

Native mudfish can survive in dried up streams or wetlands for some time.
up to 13 cm

toitoi common bully

There are several different species of native bully. They eat insect larvae, snails and worms. up to 10 cm

red-finned bully

A male red-finned bully has the job of looking after the eggs once the female has laid them. While he is looking after the eggs, the male turns black. The rest of the time it has red markings on its fins.
up to 12 cm

eels

tuna longfin eel

Adult longfin eels are only found in
New Zealand. Females can live for 80
to 100 years. Tuna have always been an
important food source for Māori. They were
also seen as guardians of rivers and lakes.
up to 2 m long, upper fin longer than the one below

tuna shortfin eel

Both longfin and shortfin
eels leave New Zealand and swim
to somewhere near Tonga where they breed
and lay their eggs before they die. The eggs
hatch into larvae that become glass eels, then
elvers. The elvers swim back to New Zealand
and up rivers to find a new home. Shortfin
eels also live in rivers in Australia
and the Pacific Islands. up to 1.2 m

pirahau lamprey

Although they look like eels, lamprey are a
different kind of fish. They have a circular,
sucking mouth rather than jaws. They can use
their mouth to hold on to rocks and even to
climb up waterfalls. up to 75 cm

introduced freshwater fish

rainbow trout

Trout were introduced to New Zealand for people who enjoy fishing. Rainbow trout can be found in large rivers and lakes. Trout are rarely found north of Auckland because the water there is too warm. up to 60 cm

brown trout

Trout eat aquatic insects such as caddisflies, they also eat other fish and kōura. Brown trout can grow bigger than rainbow trout and live in cold, running water. Because trout eat other fish, fewer native fish can survive in the same streams. up to 80 cm

koi carp

About a quarter of the fish species in our rivers and lakes are introduced. Koi carp look like giant goldfish. They are pests because they stir up the sediment in waterways, making it difficult for other animals to live there. They also compete with native fish for food and eat plants in such a way that they can't grow back.

up to 75 cm

rays & sharks

whai repo electric ray

Electric rays hunt fish and crabs at night. They stun their prey using an electric shock that they can generate from glands in their heads. 1.2 m

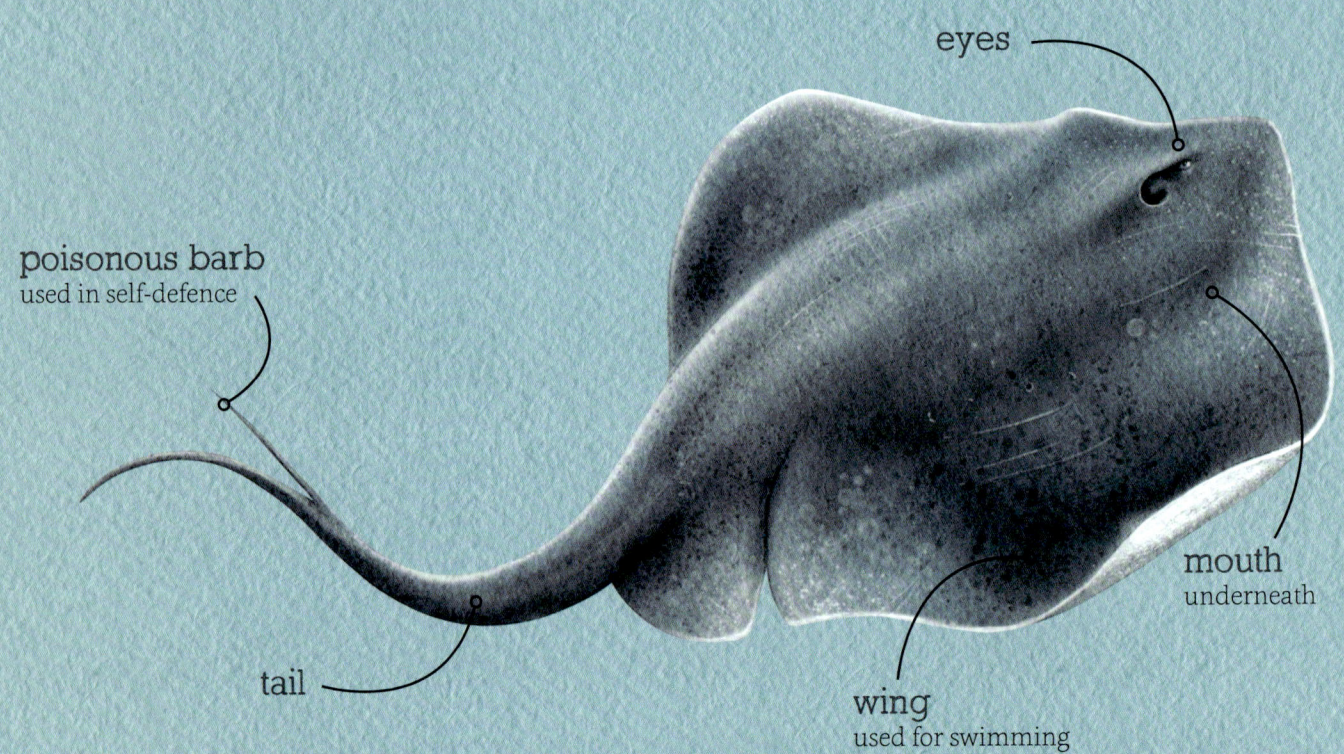

eyes

poisonous barb
used in self-defence

mouth
underneath

tail

wing
used for swimming

whai short-tailed ray

Short-tailed rays search for fish and other animals hidden in the sand. Rays live in sandy and muddy areas as well as reefs. Their flat bodies help them hide on the ocean floor. Despite their poisonous barbs they are hunted and eaten by orca. Rays and sharks are closely related. 4.3 m

pekapeka carpet shark

Carpet sharks feed at night-time and usually hide during the day. They eat fish, shellfish, octopuses and squid. Carpet sharks lay eggs but larger sharks give birth to live young. up to 1 m

mangōpare hammerhead shark

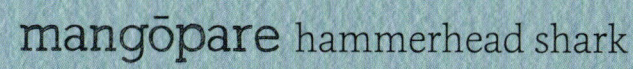

The position of the eyes of a hammerhead shark gives it 360-degree vision. Its nostrils are also on the tips of the 'hammer', which means it can smell prey more easily. up to 4 m

mako shark

Mako sharks have several rows of teeth that are replaced every few months so that they are always sharp. Sharks have always been a valuable resource for Māori and other Pacific peoples, not only for their flesh but also for their teeth. The mako shark is the fastest shark in the world and can reach speeds of over 50 kilometres an hour. up to 4 m

sharks

tupere school shark

School sharks move around in groups
or 'schools'. School sharks eat fish
and squid. up to 1.7 m

tuatini broad-nosed seven gill shark

This shark gets its English name from the seven gills
on each side – most sharks have five gills – and from
its wide head. Females grow to be a lot larger than
males; this is true for many shark species. up to 3 m

pioke rig

Rig are small sharks that live close to the coast.
They eat crab, octopus and other invertebrates
that they find in mud or sand. up to 1.5 m

Great white sharks,
also called white sharks, eat large prey
such as whales, other sharks and seals.
They can travel long distances: scientists have
tagged white sharks and tracked them
from the Chatham Islands up to Tonga,
over 3000 kilometres. up to 7 m

mangō taniwha
great white shark

hagfish

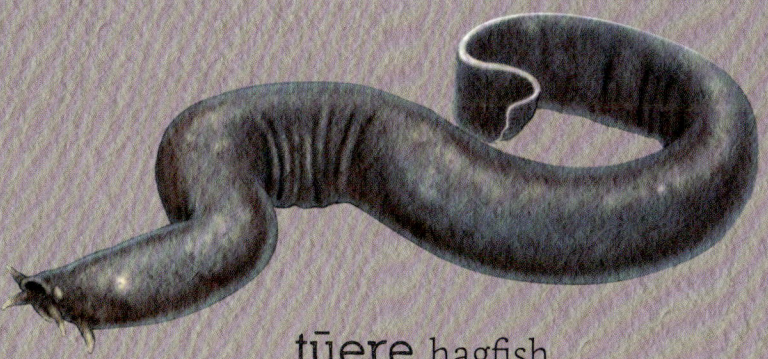

tūere hagfish

This is one fish you don't want to catch if you go fishing. When
hagfish are in danger they cover themselves in a horrible slime,
which stops predators from eating them. Hagfish, also called
blind eels, have no eyes. They find their food by smell and will
eat animals that are already dead. They suck onto their prey
and chew through the flesh. up to 1 m

saltwater fish

fins
keep fish upright and help them move through the water.

tamure snapper

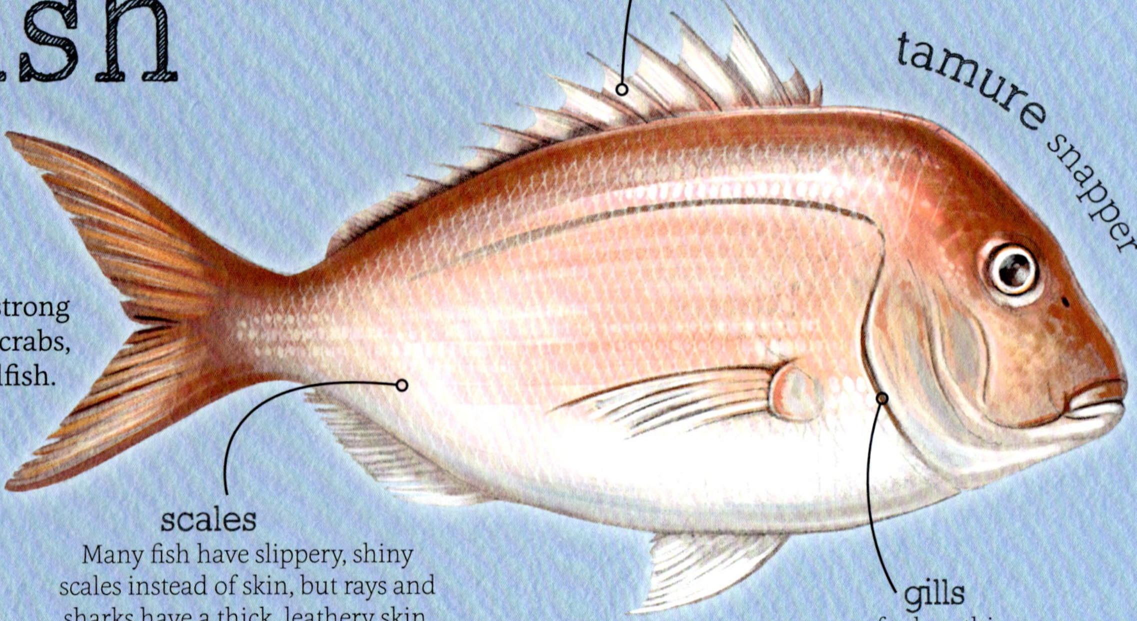

Snapper have strong teeth. They eat crabs, kina and shellfish.
up to 1.3 m

scales
Many fish have slippery, shiny scales instead of skin, but rays and sharks have a thick, leathery skin.

gills
for breathing under water

aua yellow-eyed mullet

These fish live in shallow waters at the beach, in harbours, mudflats and around mangroves. They eat algae and small animals. Predators are larger fish, and birds such as herons and kingfishers. 30 cm

pātiki flounder

Baby flounder look like other fish, but as they grow, one of their eyes moves until both eyes are on the same side. Flounder eat cockles and crabs. 45 cm

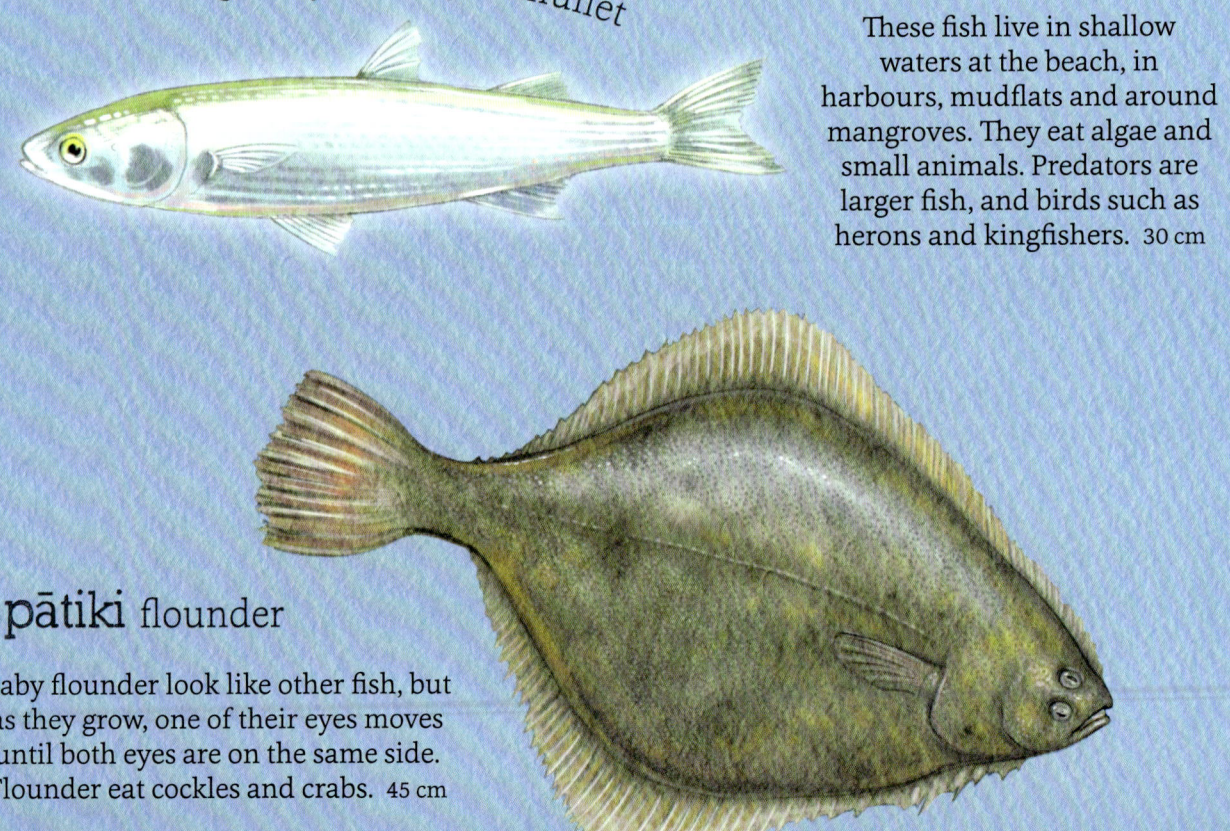

hiwihiwi kelp fish

Hiwihiwi can use their fins to hold on to rocks if the water is moving strongly around them. They eat crabs and shellfish and other invertebrates. They live around reefs and among seaweed where there are places to hide. up to 40 cm

pākirikiri blue cod

Only the larger blue cod are actually blue. Young blue cod are white with brown stripes. Blue cod live near the bottom of the sea and can rest on the sea floor standing on their fins. Their food includes shellfish, crabs and small fish. up to 60 cm

kokopu cockabully

Cockabully is the name for many different, tiny rock-pool fish. They hide between the rocks and in seaweed, and they can also bury themselves in sand. 10 cm

saltwater fish

orange roughy

Orange roughy live in the deep ocean where their large eyes make it easier for them to see. If they aren't eaten by a whale or caught in a fishing net, they can live up to 130 years. 60 cm

kōpūtōtara porcupine fish

When in danger porcupine fish suck in water until they are a round, spiky ball that would be hard to swallow. For this reason, people sometimes call them puffer fish, although real puffer fish don't have spikes. 60 cm

tuna

Tuna migrate between the warmer waters of the Pacific Ocean and the colder waters around New Zealand to feed and to breed. Seven species of tuna are found in the ocean around New Zealand. This one is a southern bluefin tuna. Tuna are fast swimmers. up to 2.2 m

bill

takeketonga marlin

Marlin eat other fish. They feed near the surface of the ocean and can use their bill to stun or kill their prey. 4 m

pouch

kiore moana
seahorse

Seahorses eat tiny animals, plankton and fish eggs. They often shelter in seaweed and use their tails to hold on to the seaweed. Female seahorses lay hundreds of eggs, which are looked after by male seahorses in their pouches. Another Māori name for seahorse is manaia. 30 cm

kaingārā moray eel

Moray eels live in caves and holes on a reef. The teeth of moray eels are sharp and curved backwards, so once they've caught a fish it can't escape. Moray eels have a second set of jaws (and teeth) inside their throats to help the eel swallow its prey. 1.5 m

saltwater fish

haku kingfish

Kingfish are one of the most common reef predators. Their silvery scales help keep them from being seen by other fish. Once they are close to their prey, they use speed to catch fish such as blue maomao and trevally. up to 1.9 m

tarakihi

Tarakihi eat brittle stars, crabs and shellfish that they find in the sand on the sea floor. At night, they rest in hollows on the sea floor. up to 70 cm

maomao blue maomao

Maomao are found in the seas around northern New Zealand. They often travel in large schools. They eat plankton, fish eggs and other small creatures. up to 40 cm

kourepoua spotted stargazer

Stargazers hide in the sand on the sea floor. Their eyes face upwards so that even when they are covered in sand they can still see. When small fish swim above them, the stargazer swings its head up, opens its mouth wide and hopes to catch its prey by surprise. up to 46 cm

matuawhāpuku scorpion fish

Scorpion fish can change colour to match their background, which is usually a rocky reef. This camouflage makes it easier for them to surprise their prey. They eat fish, crabs and other small creatures.
up to 60 cm

hāpuku groper

Hāpuku live in rocky areas where there are caves or archways. They can grow very large and can live more than 60 years. Unfortunately, fishing means few large hāpuku are now seen. They are also called hāpuka and grouper. up to 2 m

araara trevally

Trevally eat plankton, crabs, brittlestars and shellfish. A school of trevally will feed by herding plankton towards the surface, the plankton becoming trapped at the surface and are then easier to eat. up to 65 cm

seals

Seals are mammals, which means they give birth to live young.
Mothers produce milk and feed it to their young from teats.
Mammals that live in water such as seals, dolphins and
whales need to come up to the surface to breathe.

whakahao New Zealand sea lion

Sea lions like to rest on sandy beaches. Some live around
the coast of Otago and Southland but most live around
Auckland Island and Campbell Island. One of their
favourite foods is squid but they are at risk of
getting caught in the nets of boats trawling
for squid. Both the government and
fishing companies are trying to
reduce the number of
sea lions caught.

females 2 m, males 3 m

kekeno fur seal

Fur seals dive down to 200 metres for fish and
squid. In the spring they gather on rocks in breeding
colonies, where the mothers give birth to a single
pup. Fur seals live all around New Zealand.
Sometimes they rest on beaches or rocks.
All seals have sharp teeth and can move
fast on land, so it is best to keep a good
distance away from them. It is also
important to keep dogs away from
them. females 1.5 m, males 2.5 m

popoiangore leopard seal

Leopard seals have huge heads, massive jaws and very wide mouths.
While they live mostly in the Antarctic, they sometimes visit the
sea around New Zealand and will rest on beaches. They eat a wide
variety of prey including fish, fur seals, penguins and other birds.
If you are the first to see a leopard seal, elephant seal or sea lion,
the Department of Conservation will be keen to hear where
and when you saw it. up to 3.6 m

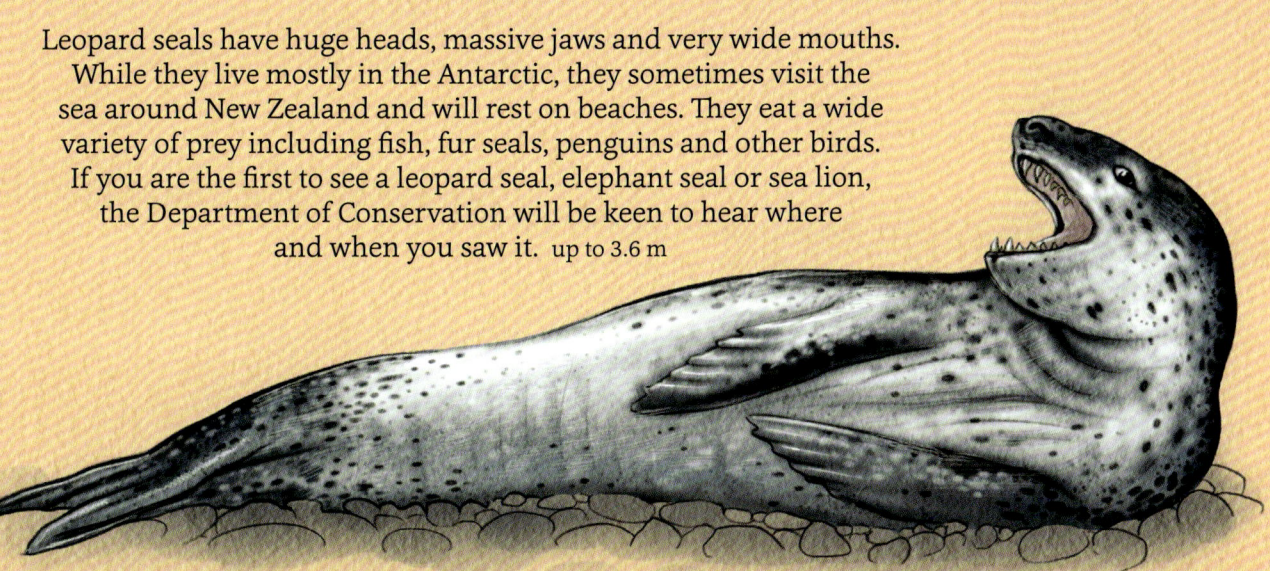

ihu koropuku
southern elephant seal

Southern elephant seals are the largest seals in the world. The males
can grow up to 5 metres long and weigh 3.6 tonnes, which is about
twice the weight of a car! Females are much smaller. They live mostly
around Auckland Island and Campbell Island but sometimes visit
the South Island and Stewart Island. Young elephant seals come
ashore to moult and will sometimes spend several months in an
area. females up to 3 m, males up to 5 m

dolphins

aihe dusky dolphin

Dusky dolphins are well known for their acrobatics. They leap right out of the water. Dolphins eat fish and squid, which they hunt using echolocation. 2 m

terehu
bottlenose dolphin

Bottlenose dolphins are seen in pods of up to 30. There are less than a thousand of them living around New Zealand. 3.5 m

aihe common dolphin

Both dusky and common dolphins sometimes come together in large schools of a thousand or more. Dolphins communicate with each other using clicks and whistles, as well as through body movements such as leaping and tail slapping. 2.6 m

tūpoupou Hector's & Maui's dolphins

These small dolphins are only found in New Zealand's seas. It is easy to tell them apart from other dolphins, as they have a rounded dorsal fin and are much smaller. Hector's dolphins are found off the coast of the South Island, and Maui's off the North Island. Both live in shallow, coastal water which puts them at risk from boats and fishing activities. Maui's dolphins are the world's rarest and smallest dolphins and are a subspecies of Hector's dolphins. 1.5 m

dorsal fin

maki orca

Some people call them killer whales, but orca are part of the dolphin family. Groups of orca come in close to shore hunting stingrays. They also hunt seals, small whales, dolphins, fish and squid. The male's dorsal fin can be up to 1.8 metres high. There are about 200 orca living around New Zealand's coast. 9 m

whales

paraōa sperm whale

Sperm whales can dive 3000 metres deep and can stay underwater for up to two hours. Whales need to come up to the surface to breathe. Sperm whales and pilot whales are toothed whales. Both use echolocation to find their prey. They make clicking noises and listen for any echoes. Echoes tell them that the sound wave has hit an object and been sent back in their direction. 18 m

upokohue
pilot whale

Pilot whales live in large family groups. They eat fish and squid and can dive up to 500 metres. Whales are sometimes found stranded on beaches. Because pilot whales live in large groups, the whole group can sometimes get stranded. Scientists are still trying to figure out why this happens. Perhaps their echolocation is confused by sandbars. 6 m

paikea humpback whale

Humpback whales travel through New Zealand's
oceans on their way between Antarctic waters and the
Pacific. There are many Māori legends about whales.
In some, Paikea is the whale rider, saved by whales
when he was tipped out of his canoe. 13 m

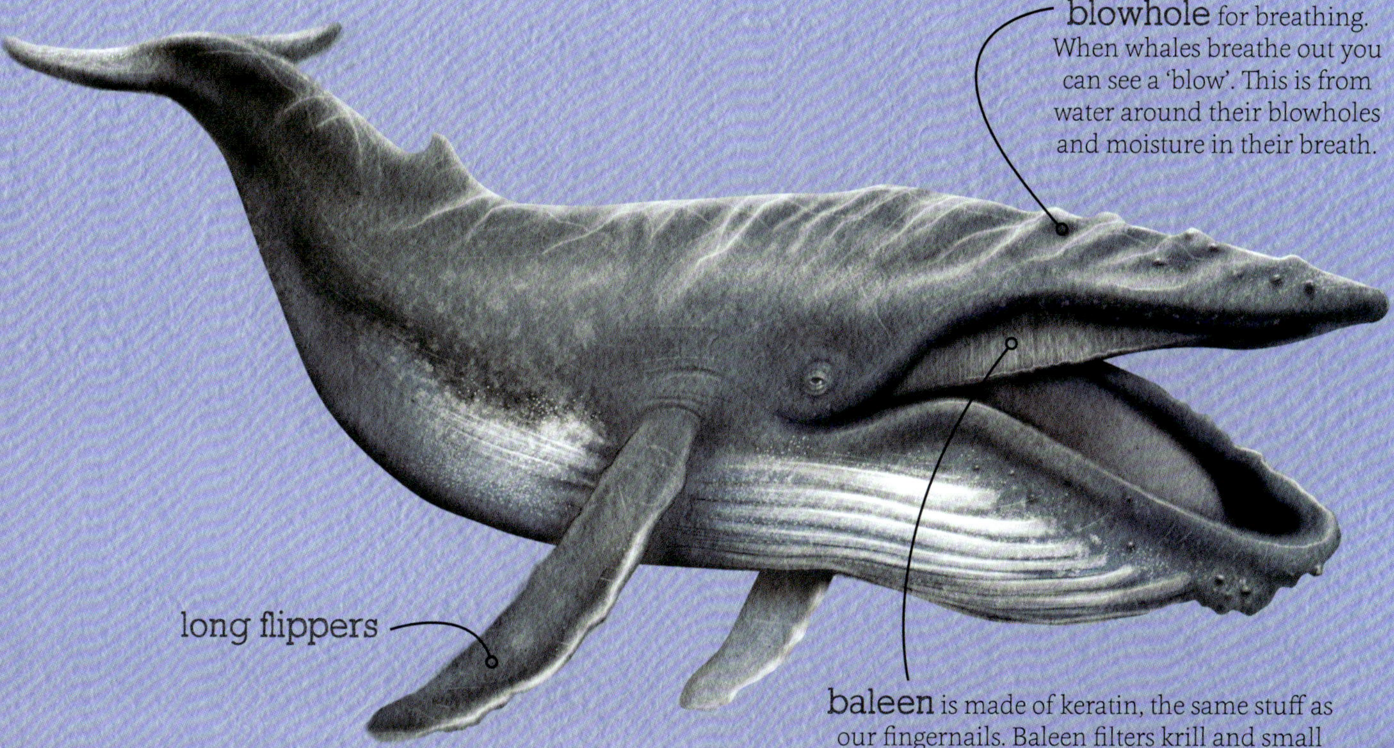

blowhole for breathing.
When whales breathe out you
can see a 'blow'. This is from
water around their blowholes
and moisture in their breath.

long flippers

baleen is made of keratin, the same stuff as
our fingernails. Baleen filters krill and small
fish out of the water for the whale to eat. Other
baleen whales include blue whales, Bryde's
whale and right whales (pages 66–67).

hakurā
Gray's beaked whale

Eleven species of beaked whales are found around New Zealand.
They all have long, pointy jaws that look like beaks. Not much is
known about beaked whales because they are rarely seen at sea.
Most of the information scientists have about them is from whales
found stranded on beaches. The Gray's beaked whale is the most
commonly stranded beaked whale. They eat squid. up to 6 m

whales

tohorā blue whale

tohorā right whale

no fin
on top

Named by European
whalers because they
were the 'right' or
easiest whales to catch,
they were almost extinct
when New Zealand stopped
whaling in the 1960s. 17 m

Blue whales are the largest animals in the world. They are baleen whales – the baleen acts like a net to filter out krill (page 81). They need to eat huge amounts of krill, perhaps up to 40 million a day. The blue whales seen around New Zealand migrate to the Antarctic in summer. Blue whales don't use echolocation but they do make loud calls or songs which help them find each other. Despite blue whales being so large, scientists are still making discoveries about where they live and feed. up to 30 m

Bryde's whale

Bryde's is pronounced 'brood-ers'. These whales prefer warm water and live in the ocean around the north of the North Island. Scientists have found that Bryde's whales spend most of their time in the top 10 metres of the ocean. Unfortunately, this means they may get hit and killed by boats or ships. 14 m

native bats

Bats are New Zealand's only native land mammals.

the **bat fly** lives with short-tailed bats. It eats bat poo and hitches a ride on the bat's fur.

pekapeka short-tailed bat

Bats are nocturnal. Short-tailed bats can crawl on the ground using their folded-up wings like legs. This unusual habit helps them find nectar and fruit but puts them at risk from predators. Thousands of short-tailed bats roost together during the daytime. Bats roost in holes in large old trees, so it's important to leave these trees standing. Sadly, bats are now quite rare in New Zealand.

wingspan up to 30 cm, body length 4–6 cm

pekapeka long-tailed bat

The long-tailed bat lives in roosts of up to 100 bats. They move roost sites often. They eat flying insects such as moths and beetles.

wingspan up to 30 cm, body length 4–6 cm

introduced mammals

Mustelid is the name given to mammals such as stoats, weasels and ferrets. Other mustelids not found in New Zealand include badgers and otters. The mustelids on this page were brought to New Zealand to hunt rabbits, however, they found it much easier to hunt native birds, lizards and insects.

weasel tori uaroa

Weasels are less common than stoats. But like stoats they eat birds, birds' eggs, lizards and insects. up to 22 cm

stoat toriura

Stoats hunt day or night, killing whatever they find even if they aren't hungry. They hunt using sound and smell to find birds, eggs, lizards and insects. They can swim more than 1.5 kilometres, which means they can swim to some islands. Stoats have a black tip on the end of their tail; weasels don't. 35–40 cm

ferret tori hura

Ferrets are the largest mustelid found in New Zealand. They are capable of killing kiwi, whio and penguins. Their main food is rabbits, but if rabbit numbers are low they will eat rats, possums and birds. up to 46 cm

introduced mammals

hedgehog tuatete

Hedgehogs eat invertebrates, lizards and birds' eggs. They use their prickles as a defence, rolling up into a ball of prickles if they feel threatened. You might hear them snuffling in your garden at night, but you can also see them during the day. In cold areas they hibernate, or sleep all through winter. This is how they can survive cold weather. 30–38 cm

mouse kiore

Mice can get through very small gaps, which means that they will often find a way to get into people's houses. They eat seeds and berries as well as insects and worms. up to 20 cm including tail

rat kiore

There are three different kinds of rat in New Zealand: the Pacific rat, the Norway rat and the ship rat. If you see rats in your garden, they are most likely ship rats. They are good climbers and will try to nest in house roofs. Rats are omnivores, which means they eat plants as well as animals. They eat seeds, fruit, birds, insects, lizards, snails, birds' eggs and so on. up to 46 cm including tail

feral cat ngeru

Feral cats are cats that live completely in the wild. Their ancestors were probably domestic cats left alone by their owners. As only the best hunters could survive, after several generations they became bigger than domestic cats. Feral cats eat all sorts of animals including rabbits, birds, birds' eggs, bats and lizards. Cats are responsible for the extinction of several native birds including the Stephen's Island wren. up to 7 kg

possum paihamu

Possums are marsupials – mammals that keep their young in a pouch until they are big enough to leave. Possums were brought to New Zealand from Australia and they love eating the New Zealand bush. Their main diet is leaves, flowers and fruit but they have also been seen eating birds and birds' eggs. They are nocturnal animals, which means they are active at night-time.
up to 95 cm long

rabbit rāpeti

Rabbits were brought to New Zealand for people to eat and to use their fur. Some rabbits went wild and the wild population grew quickly because there were few predators. Farmers consider rabbits to be pests because they eat grass that sheep or cattle need. They are most often seen in the evening and are active at night. 50 cm

introduced mammals

Kaimanawa wild horse
hōiho

Wild horses live in the Kaimanawa area of the central North Island. The horses can damage the unique native plants that live here so the number in the herd is kept at around 300 horses. This also means they are healthier, because if there were too many horses, they would not find enough to eat and would starve.

up to 1.5 m high

feral pig poaka

Pigs dig up the ground looking for plant roots, insects and snails. They also wallow in mud. Wallows and diggings are among the signs that pigs leave in the bush. up to 2.2 m long

fallow deer pikareka

All deer are herbivores – they eat plants such as grass, ferns and tree leaves. Deer can damage native forests, making it hard for some plants to grow. Fallow deer are small deer that are found in both the North and South islands.

up to 1 m high

feral goat nanenane

Like pigs and horses, feral goats are descended from tame animals that have gone wild. Goats are good climbers and can also stand up on their back legs to reach leaves that are up to 2 metres high.
up to 68 cm high

Himalayan tahr

Tahr (also spelled thar) are closely related to goats. Although originally from the Himalayas, they were brought to New Zealand from England. Tahr are amazing climbers and live up high in the Southern Alps. Their thick coat keeps them warm in the snow.
up to 1 m high

red deer tia

There are seven different species of deer in New Zealand. They were brought here from Asia, Europe and North America for people to hunt. Red deer are the most common deer in New Zealand.
up to 1.9 m long, male, 1.8 m long, female

microscopic
animals

plankton

Plankton are the most important food source in the ocean, but they are so small you need a microscope to see them. There are two main types of plankton floating around in the ocean: phytoplankton, which are like tiny plants, and zooplankton, which are tiny animals that eat other plankton.

other microscopic life

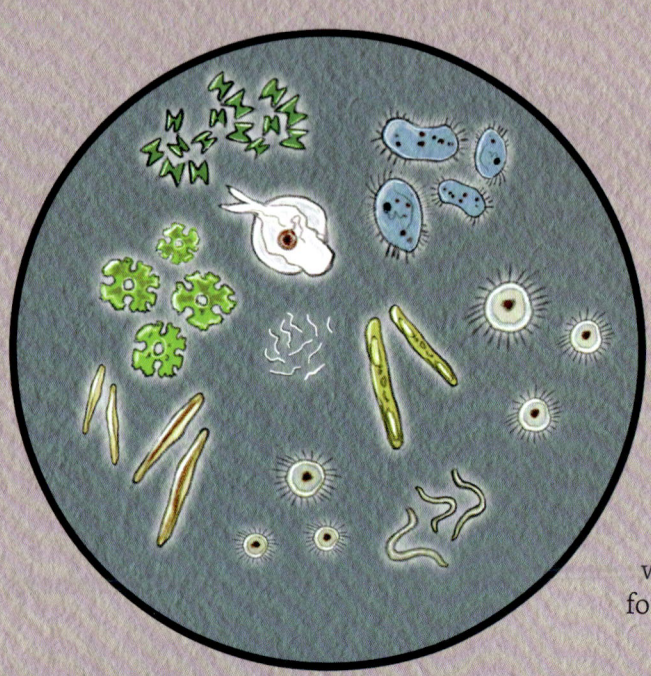

There are lots of microscopic things living in fresh water, too. They include tiny animals, bacteria and algae. Other microscopic animals can be found living on land, such as dust mites that live in houses but are too small to see without a microscope. Microscopic life plays an important role as part of the ecosystem, wherever it is. Some eat plant material, which helps get rid of dead plants, some provide food for other animals, which in turn provides food for larger animals.

worms

ngāokeoke peripatus

Sometimes called velvet worms, these strange creatures are not true worms. They have between 13 and 16 pairs of stumpy legs and can be purple, blue, brown or mottled depending on the species. They catch their insect or centipede prey with a sticky fluid, and then suck the juice out of the prey. They breathe through the pores in their skin. up to 80 mm

toke worm

Worms don't have bones. Their body segments have muscles that help them move. If you see a bump around its middle, this is where the worm is storing its eggs. Garden worms like living in soil and compost. They eat decaying plant material. Some native worms that live in the soil of forests can grow over 1 metre long.

tubeworm

There are over 500 different species of tubeworm in the oceans around New Zealand. They build a tube to live in and extend their feathery tentacles out of the tube to catch plankton for food.

spiders

The Māori name for spiders is pūngāwerewere. Spiders all have eight legs and several body segments. They are part of a large group of animals called arthropods. Arthropod means 'jointed leg', something they all have in common. They are also all invertebrates, that is they don't have bones. Other arthropods are crustaceans, insects, centipedes and millipedes.

daddy long-legs spider

You might find these spiders in your house, as they like to make their webs in the corners of rooms. If another spider or insect gets caught in the web, the daddy long-legs spider quickly wraps more silk around it, wrapping it up until the prey can't move anymore. It often leaves these food parcels to eat later. legs up to 50 mm long

nursery web spider

The female nursery web spider makes a web to protect its babies. About 200 baby spiders are kept safe in the web until they are big enough to leave.
18 mm

water spider

Water spiders don't live in the water but beside it. They use their legs to feel for vibrations of struggling insects and can walk on water to reach their prey. A close relative of nursery web spiders, water spiders spin their webs among stones to protect their young.
6 cm, including legs

wolf spider

orbweb spider

The orbweb spider makes a sticky web to catch insects. You might wonder why it doesn't get stuck in its own web. It covers its legs with an oily liquid so it can't get caught. Once the orbweb spider has caught an insect, it wraps it up to eat later. 12 mm

Wolf spiders don't build webs to live in or to catch prey; instead they go hunting. Female wolf spiders carry their eggs around with them and, when the baby spiders hatch, they carry them around too. 7 mm

tunnel web spider

Tunnel web spiders build a web inside a hole. They hide inside the tunnel waiting for an insect to walk across their web.
2.5 cm

The katipō is New Zealand's only venomous native spider. Katipō live on beaches, among driftwood and grasses. They are now extremely rare so it's unlikely you will come across one. However, two Australian venomous spiders are now found in New Zealand: redback spider and white-tailed spider. Some other spiders bite as well, so it's best to leave them alone. body up to 8 mm

katipō spider

77

crabs

Crabs are part of a group of arthropods called crustaceans that also includes crayfish, krill and shrimps. Crustaceans have a shell-like covering that protects their body and their head. In order to grow they need to moult, to shed their old shell, and a new larger shell grows in its place.

king crab

These huge crabs live deep down on the sea floor, up to 1.5 kilometres below the ocean surface. Crabs have a good sense of smell, which helps them find food in dark places such as the ocean floor. up to 1 m

pāpaka nui purple or shore crab

Purple rock crabs live in rock pools. They hide under rocks during the day and scuttle around looking for food at night. Crabs can breathe under water as well as out of water. 4 cm

kāunga waerau hermit crab

Hermit crabs don't have a hard carapace like other crabs, so they look for an empty shell to live in. When they grow, they move into a bigger shell. 3 cm

camouflage crab pāpaka huna

Camouflage crabs have a clever way of hiding in the rock pools. They use their claws to stick seaweed and sponges on to their shells so they look like rocks. 2 cm

half crab kawekawe

You might think that half crabs have lost some legs but they grow this way. They hide under rocks or between stones and eat by filtering out tiny pieces of food from the water. 2 cm

kairau mud crab

Mud crabs are the colour of mud, which makes it easy for them to hide. They eat seaweed and plant material. 3 cm

pāpaka paddle crab

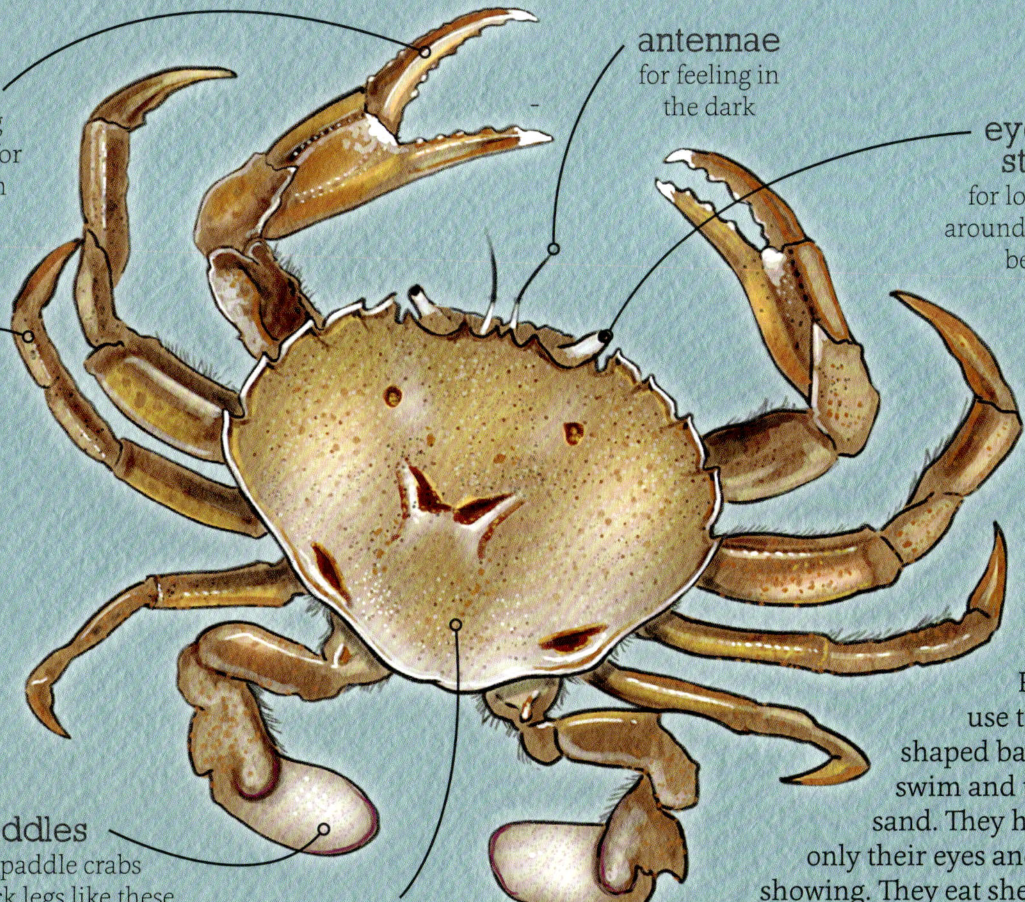

claws
for defending themselves or for breaking open shells

antennae
for feeling in the dark

eyes on stalks
for looking all around, including behind

legs
The joints in crabs' legs make it easier for them to walk sideways.

paddles
Only paddle crabs have back legs like these for swimming and digging.

carapace
This hard shell protects the crab's soft body.

Paddle crabs use their paddle-shaped back legs to swim and to dig into sand. They hide with only their eyes and antennae showing. They eat shellfish, such as pipi and tuatua, which they break open with their claws. 10 cm

other crustaceans

kōura freshwater crayfish

gills

Kōura are native freshwater crayfish.
They help to keep streams clean by
scavenging for food, such as leaves and insects,
on the riverbed. Female kōura carry their eggs
around with them. When they hatch, baby
kōura hang on to their mother until they
are about 4 millimetres long. 7–8 cm long

slater

These strange-looking creatures, also called
woodlice, are one of the few crustaceans that live
out of water. They eat dead plant material so do a
good job of cleaning up in the garden. They can
only live where it is wet or damp. up to 17 mm

barnacle

Perhaps the most surprising crustacean is the barnacle.
It stays in one place attached to a surface. The shell-like
plates of barnacles open for feeding when the tide is
in and close when it goes out. They can live on other
shells, rocks, boats and even whales. up to 2 cm

sandhopper mōwhitiwhiti

If you move seaweed on the beach, you might see
lots of sandhoppers jumping around. They can
jump up to 30 centimetres. 1 cm

crayfish kōura papatea

Crayfish can live up to 30 years and grow up to 3 kilograms. They shed their shell every few months and grow a new one. Crayfish are predators and hunt at night. They are known to travel large distances on the sea floor. up to 50 cm

krill kōura rangi

Krill are shrimp-like creatures just a few centimetres long. Despite being so tiny they are the main food of the sea's largest animals, the baleen whales. A blue whale can eat over 3 tonnes of krill a day. Krill are also eaten by seabirds and fish.

shrimp kōura rangi

It can be hard to spot shrimps in a rock pool because they are small and transparent (you can almost see through them.) Shrimps use their long antennae to feel for food. There are fresh-water shrimps too, which are found in rivers and lakes. 2 cm

antennae

butterflies & moths

Butterflies and moths are insects and their Māori name is pūrerehua. Insects come in all shapes and sizes. Their young can look quite different from the adult, like caterpillars and butterflies. One thing they have in common is that the adults of all insects have six legs. All the animals on pages 82–94 are insects.

from egg to butterfly

eggs butterflies and moths lay their eggs on plants that the caterpillar can eat.

anuhe caterpillar caterpillars (also called larvae) hatch out of the eggs. They eat and eat until they are ready to form a chrysalis.

kahuku monarch butterfly, caterpillar & chrysalis

tūngoungou chrysalis the caterpillar stops eating and becomes a chrysalis. Inside the chrysalis it changes into a butterfly or moth.

butterfly the butterfly emerges from the chrysalis and flys off to find a mate. The female lays eggs and the cycle starts again.

Monarch butterflies lay their eggs on swan plants or other plants in the milkweed family.
wingspan up to 100 mm

kahukura red admiral butterfly

This native butterfly is sometimes seen in gardens. It lays its eggs on the native nettle onga onga. Onga onga gives people a very nasty sting, but the caterpillars don't have any problems touching it and eating it. wingspan 50–60 mm

common blue butterfly

This butterfly can often be seen on lawns where clover is growing. wingspan 17–27 mm

cabbage tree moth

The stripes on a cabbage tree moth are good camouflage. When the moth is lying on a leaf of the cabbage tree or tī kōuka, the stripes match those on the leaf. The caterpillars of this moth eat the leaves, leaving large grooves or holes behind them as they munch through. wingspan 35 mm

cabbage butterfly & caterpillar

Gardeners think cabbage butterflies are pests. The cabbage butterfly lays its eggs on cabbage and broccoli, and the caterpillars spend about four to five weeks eating the plants before they turn into a chrysalis. They were introduced to New Zealand by mistake! wingspan 45–50 mm

moths

bag moth
pū a Raukatari

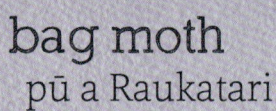

The bag moth is most unusual. The female never leaves the bag, in fact she has no wings. The caterpillar makes a bag to live in and moves around carrying its bag. It goes through the chrysalis stage in its bag. Only if it's a male, does it turn into a moth with wings.

bag length 6 cm

pepetuna pūriri moth

The caterpillar of the pūriri moth make holes in pūriri trees, putaputaweta trees and some others. Once inside the tree it creates a soft, silk cover for the hole. It spends months or even years eating the tree. It goes through the chrysalis stage in the hole. Pepetuna is the largest moth in New Zealand. It lives for only two days, long enough to mate and lay eggs. This is a female moth; the male has plainer wings. Pepetuna is found only in North Island forests. wingspan 15 cm

mōkarakara
magpie moth

This moth flies around during the daytime. Its caterpillars are often called 'woolly bear' caterpillars or makokōrori.

wingspan 4.5 cm

wētā

cave wētā

Wētā are only found in New Zealand. They are nocturnal. Cave wētā can be found during the day in caves or other dark, damp places. At night, they come out into the forest to eat. Thanks to their long back legs, cave wētā can jump 2 or 3 metres. length, including legs and antennae, 3.5 cm

giant wētā

There are 11 different species of giant wētā. The largest is the wētāpunga from Little Barrier Island. Wētāpunga means 'god of ugly things'. Although they are large, and might be considered ugly, they are not aggressive. They eat plants. Giant wētā are one of the world's heaviest insects, weighing up to 35 grams. Giant wētā are quite rare and are now mostly found in sanctuaries or on predator-free islands. up to 10 cm

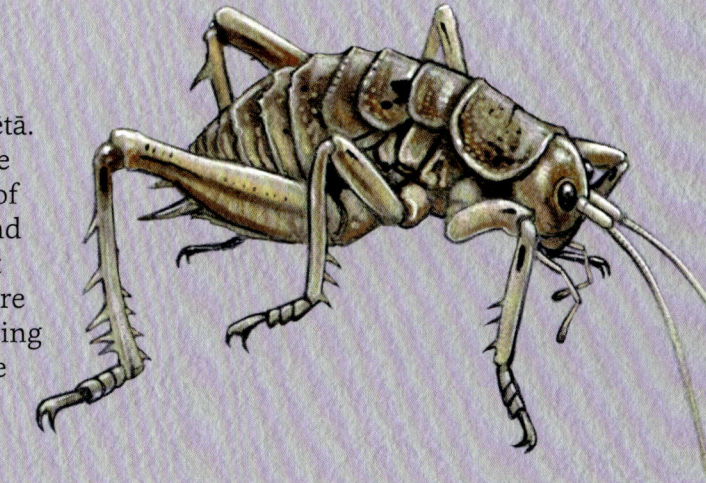

scree wētā

The scree wētā is a giant wētā that lives in the mountains. They freeze in the cold weather but still survive once they've thawed out. 5 cm

tree wētā

Tree wētā fight and will lift up their spiky legs if they feel threatened. The spike on the back end of this female tree wētā is an ovipositor, which helps it to lay eggs. 4 cm

bees, wasps flies & ants

bumblebee

Bumblebees live in smaller groups than honeybees. They usually make their nest in holes in the ground or in trees. They are the only bee with a tongue long enough to get nectar from red clover, and this is why people brought them to New Zealand. 25 mm

pollen bags

honey bee pi

Honeybees are social insects – they live together in large groups. Each beehive has one queen, some drones (male bees) and hundreds of worker bees. The worker bees collect nectar and pollen from flowers. They make wax to build their nest and for storing honey. Honeybees use dances to tell each other where to find flowers. 12 mm

sting

common wasp
wāpi

Watch out for wasps! They like sugary food and drinks, so make sure they aren't sharing yours. Wasps eat insects and spiders too. They don't collect pollen or make honey. They nest in warm places, such as sunny banks or even in house roofs. 20 mm

ngaro huruhuru native bee

There are many species of native bees. Most live on their own in holes they make in the ground. Unlike honey bees, they don't make honey that people can collect. up to 12 mm

paper wasp

The nests of paper wasps look like they are made from paper, which is how they get their name. Paper wasps fly with their back legs hanging down, unlike common wasps that tuck their legs in. Paper wasps can sting. up to 15 mm

ant pōpokorua

Ants live in colonies, and each ant has a different role in the colony. There is usually only one queen ant, but there are many soldiers, nurses and workers. Ants are very strong. They can carry up to 50 times their own weight. They are scavengers and will eat dead insects as well as sugary foods. up to 10 mm

drone fly

Looks like a bee? Look carefully and you can see that the orange stripes of a drone fly do not always join across its back. Drone flies don't sting but they do eat nectar and pollen. 13 mm

housefly rango

Flies have a good sense of smell, which helps them find food and places to lay their eggs. They do this on rotting food or plants so that the young maggots will have food to eat when they hatch. 8 mm

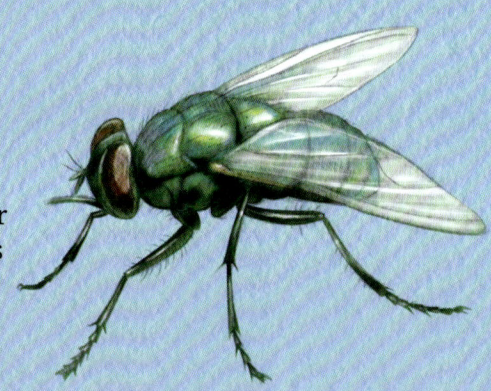

beetles & bugs

huhu beetle

The larvae of this beetle are called huhu grubs. They live in rotting trees. Māori found them to be good to eat. The adult beetles are active at night and are sometimes attracted to house lights. 40–50 mm

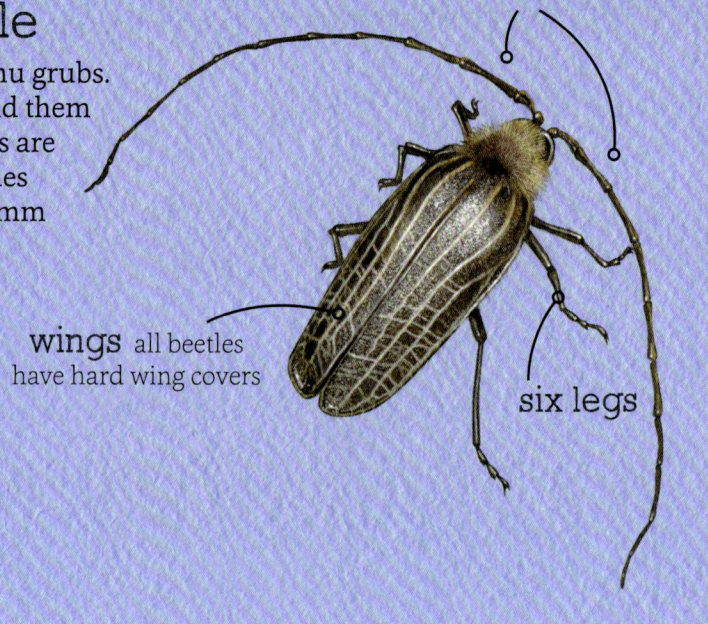

two antennae

wings all beetles have hard wing covers

six legs

bronze beetle tutaeruru

The larvae of bronze beetles are grass grubs. Grass grubs live in the earth eating the roots of grass. The adult beetles feed on leaves and fruit. 1 cm

ladybird mumutawa

Ladybirds can be red, yellow or orange. The bright colours of ladybirds tell birds and other possible predators that they are poisonous to eat. Ladybirds are beetles that can fly. up to 5 mm

diving beetle

aphid

Aphids suck juice from plants. They breed quickly and there can be quite large numbers on a plant. They are a favourite food of birds, praying mantises and ladybirds. up to 2–4 mm

Diving beetles need to breathe air, so they trap air bubbles under their wings, which allows them to stay underwater for longer. 1 cm

water boatman
hoehoe tuara

Water boatmen are commonly
found on the surface of still water.
They eat algae. They use their legs
like oars, for moving across water.
under 1 cm

stag beetle

There are many different stag beetles
in New Zealand; not all of them can
fly. Some stag beetles eat rotting
wood, but others are thought to eat
nectar or sap. up to 44 mm

back swimmer
hoe tuara

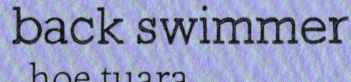

These insects get their name from the fact
that they lie on their backs to swim.
They eat prey such as tadpoles
and small fish. under 1 cm

giraffe weevil
tūwhaipapa

Although they are commonly called weevils,
these insects are flying beetles. The male has a
long head that is half the total length of its body.
Females have much shorter heads. Adult
giraffe weevils feed on sap from trees.
male up to 70 mm, female 45 mm

other insects

kihikihi cicada

In summer, cicadas emerge from the ground, climb out of their old skins and fly off to find a mate. Male cicadas sing to attract females. They vibrate their bodies to make their song.

up to 40 mm including wings

grasshopper kōhiti

Grasshoppers use their back legs to make huge jumps, jumping 20 times their body length. Male grasshoppers make a chirping sound by rubbing their legs against their wings. Grasshoppers eat grass! up to 20 mm

stick insect rō

Stick insects can be green or brown, smooth or rough. They feed on leaves at night. During the day they stay quite still so birds can't see them. up to 200 mm including its front legs.

silverfish

Silverfish are sometimes found in houses. They eat anything with starch in it. Because paper is made from starchy wood fibres, they will eat paper in books, photos and wallpaper.

up to 15 mm

praying mantis rō

The praying mantis is a predator. It uses its camouflage to pretend to be a leaf, then it jumps suddenly onto its prey. It eats flies, aphids and other insects. You might find its egg case on a fence or branch.
30–40 mm including its wings

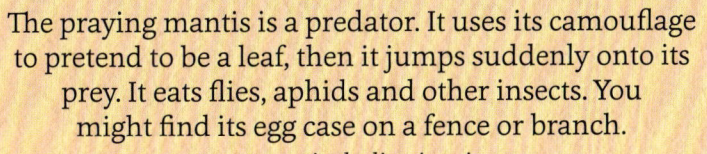

egg case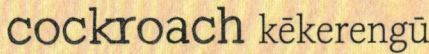

cockroach kēkerengū

Native cockroaches live in the bush or among stones and leaf litter. Some introduced cockroaches live in houses, where they can be pests because they eat food scraps. up to 40 mm

earwig hiore kakati

Earwigs eat plants, fruit and other insects. They use their pincers for grabbing and holding insect prey. There are lots of different stories about how earwigs got their strange English name – but don't worry, they aren't interested in your ears! 10–20 mm

green planthopper
kiritaitea

These insects are camouflaged to look like leaves. They feed on the juice of plants. up to 10 mm

aquatic insects

Aquatic insects live part of their life underwater in streams, rivers and lakes. Only their adult life is spent above water. The young aquatic insects are called nymphs or larvae. They can breathe underwater using gills.

adult

mayfly piriwai

Adult mayflies have such a short life that they don't need to eat! Mayfly nymphs live for several months underwater eating algae and other plant material.
wingspan up to 3 cm

nymph

sandfly namu

The female sandfly needs a meal of blood to help develop her eggs. She will bite animals such as birds, seals and humans. Males don't bite. Sandflies are usually only active during the day as they cannot see at night. up to 3 mm

mosquito waeroa

Only the female mosquito takes blood. There are several different species, one makes a high-pitched buzzing sound and bites at night, others are silent and bite during the day. Mosquitoes and sandflies both need water to lay their eggs and for their larvae to live in. up to 5 mm

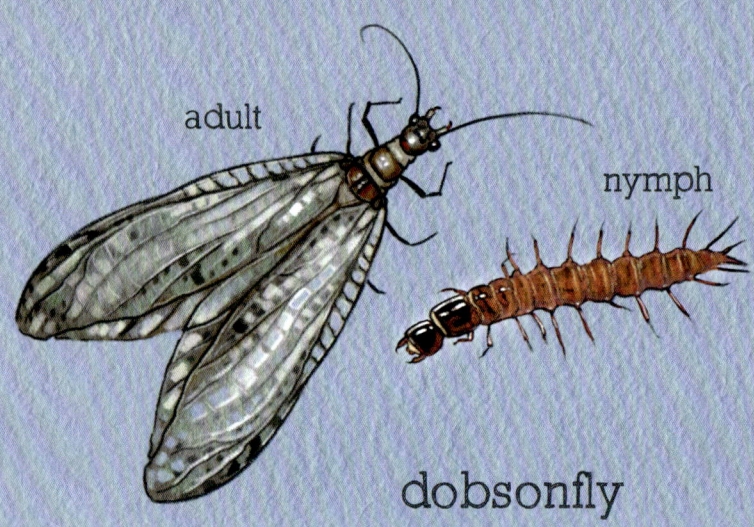

adult

nymph

dobsonfly

Look under a stone in a river or stream and you might find a dobsonfly nymph. They are one of the most commonly found aquatic insects and are often called 'toebiters'. over 2 cm long

caddisfly

There are over 200 species of caddisfly. Some caddisfly larvae make cases out of silk, which they attach to rocks underwater to keep from being swept downstream.

adult up to 8 cm long

adult

nymph

stonefly

Like many other aquatic insects, stonefly nymphs can only live in healthy streams. Scientists count insect species to measure the health of waterways. up to 2.5 cm

nymph

adult

nymph
4–5 cm

damselfly

Damselflies eat other insects which they catch on the wing (while flying). They fold their wings together when they land (dragonflies don't).

up to 4.5 cm long

giant dragonfly
kapowai

Dragonfly nymphs live underwater for several years, eating other insect larvae. Adult dragonflies are fast flyers, catching other insects on the wing (while flying).

10–12 cm wingspan

more insects

beech scale insect

Beech scale insects live in the bark of beech trees, sucking on the sap and pooing out honeydew through a long, thread-like tube at their rear end. A sooty-mould fungus grows on the honeydew, which is what makes some beech trees look black.

honeydew is an important food source for birds such as kākā, tūī, bellbirds, as well as for geckos and insects.

flea puruhi

There are several different species of fleas. Fleas live on a host animal, for example, cats, birds and dogs. Fleas need the blood of the host animal to live and breed. If they are very hungry then they'll bite humans too. Fleas are amazing jumpers – they can jump 50 times their body length. up to 5 mm

glow-worm titiwai

Glow-worms aren't worms – they are the larvae of a kind of fly. At night the larvae's tail glows to attract insects to sticky threads that it has let down to catch prey. Glow-worms are found in damp places such as caves or banks of streams. 20 mm

crane fly
mate waeroa

Because they have such long legs, people sometimes confuse crane flies with daddy long-legs spiders. But look carefully and you can see that crane flies have wings and only six legs. Adult crane flies don't live long; some eat nectar, others don't eat at all. The larvae of crane flies live in rotting wood or the ground. up to 3 cm

centipedes & millipedes

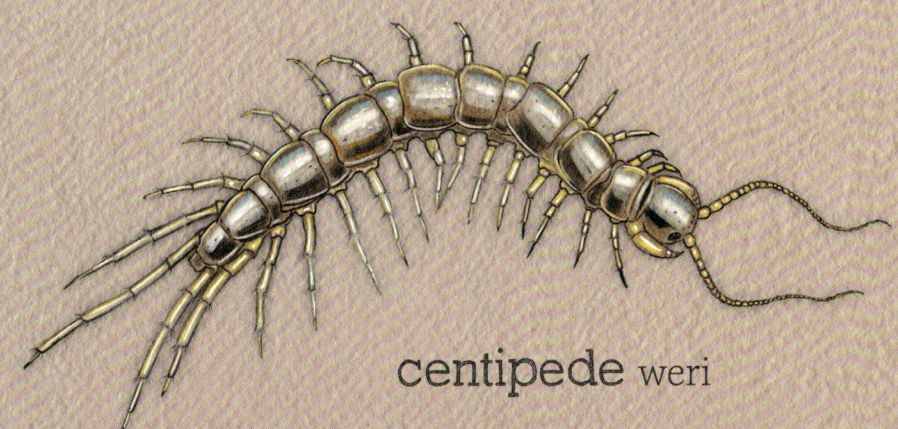

centipede weri

All centipedes are carnivorous – they eat insects,
worms and slugs. They kill their prey using
claws on their front legs, and their bite can be
painful to humans. There is a giant centipede
that can grow up to 20 centimetres long, which
is found in logs or among leaves. up to 100 mm

millipede weri

Millipedes are vegetarian – they eat plant
material. They have lots of legs, although not as
many as their name suggests. If you look closely,
you can see that centipedes have one pair of legs
under each segment and millipedes have two.
up to 100 mm

jellyfish & sponges

ihumoana
blue bottle

These are not real jellyfish. They are a group of tiny animals living under a floating blue air bag. Don't touch dead blue bottles on the beach because their tentacles sting, even when they are dead. 5 cm

lion's mane jellyfish

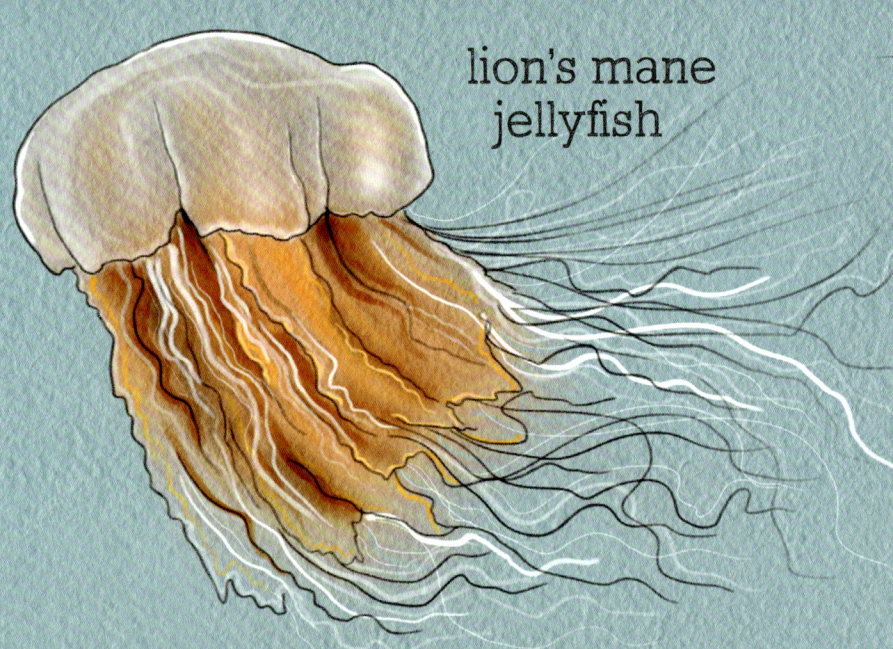

This jellyfish is named for its long tentacles which people thought resembled a lion's mane. The tentacles sting, so it's best to avoid the lion's mane jellyfish. Jellyfish are eaten by seabirds, turtles and large fish. up to 1 m across

petipeti
common jellyfish

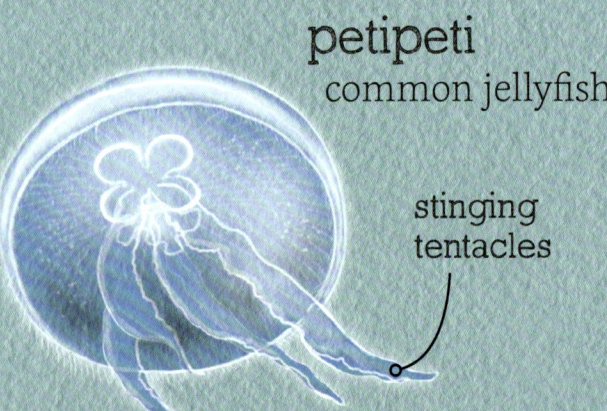

stinging tentacles

The common jellyfish is also called the moon jellyfish. This jellyfish eats tiny animals, which it catches with its stinging tentacles. Its sting doesn't hurt people. 20 cm

finger sponge
pūngorungoru

pores

Sponges pull sea water through their pores, they filter out food and push the water out again. Living sponges are bright yellow; this one is a dead one that washed up on the beach.

anemones
& coral

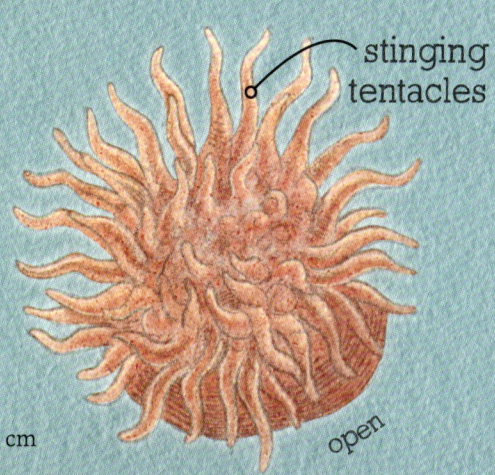

stinging
tentacles

kōtore moana sea anemone

closed

These sea anemones like to live on rocks where there is no sun or wind. They close up when the tide goes out and open again when they are covered by water. They move by sliding along the rock. 2 cm

open

wandering sea anemone

Wandering sea anemones float in the water but can also hold onto rocks or kelp to stay in one place. The best time to see them is at night, when they move around looking for food. 20 cm

lace coral or bryozoans

The tiny animals that make up lace coral feed on plankton. They build a structure to live in that looks like a shell or skeleton. Lace corals can't move so they rely on the ocean currents to bring food to them. There are about 950 species of lace coral around New Zealand.

sea stars

All the animals on this page and page 97 are closely related. Sea stars (also called starfish), kina, sea cucumbers and sand dollars are all echinoderms. Echinoderm means 'spiny skin', which is a good description of the outside of a kina.

weki huna brittle star

Brittle stars usually have five arms, which they use to crawl along the sea floor as well as to catch food. 12 cm

spines
for protection

tube feet
for moving around and
holding onto rocks

piece of dead kina shell
spines have fallen off

kina sea urchin

Kina eat seaweed, such as kelp. They are eaten by fish and sea stars, and people like to eat them too. Between their spines are long tube feet. 10 cm

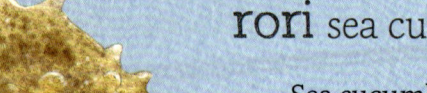

rori sea cucumber

Sea cucumbers have tube feet to help them walk. They vacuum up mud and sediment from the ocean floor, filtering out the food before pooing the rest out. up to 12 cm

kapu parahua cushion star

Cushion stars are small sea stars that have four to six arms. They are scavengers and will eat small animals, such as barnacles. 7 cm

kina pākira sand dollar

Sand dollars are a bit like a flattened kina. Their flat shape makes it easier to burrow into mud and sand. Like the sea cucumber they eat food they find in the mud. 10 cm

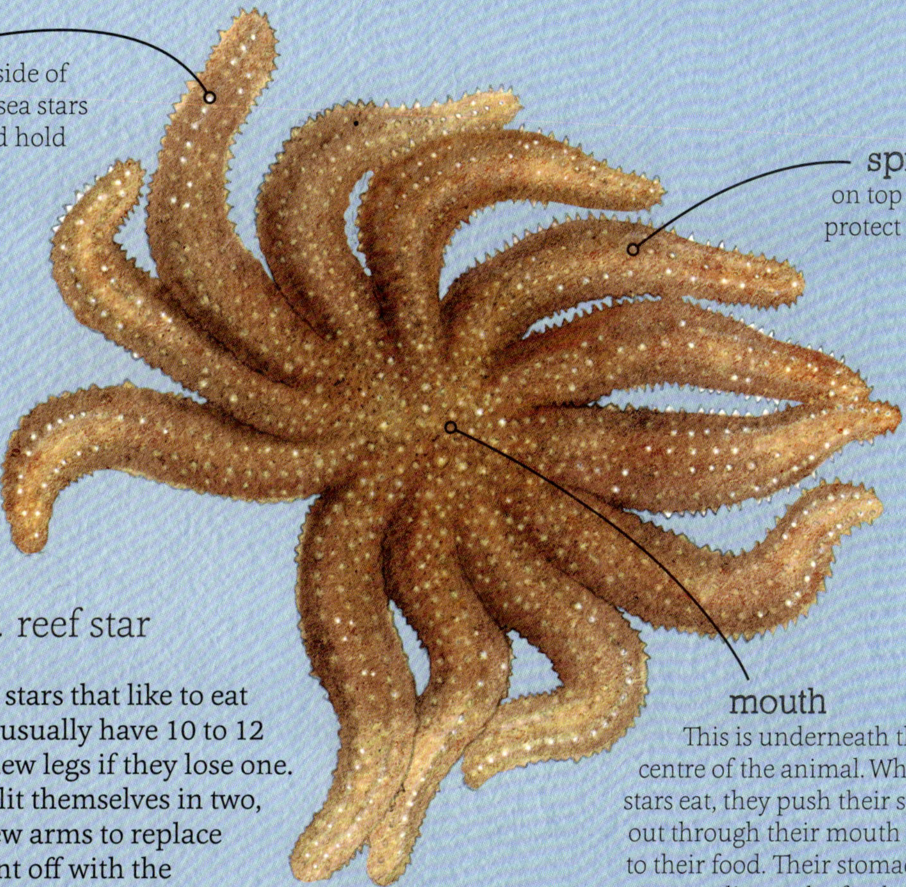

suckers
are on the underside of the arms and help sea stars move around and hold onto rocks.

spines
on top of the arms protect the reef star.

pātangaroa reef star

Reef stars are large sea stars that like to eat mussels and kina. They usually have 10 to 12 arms. Sea stars can grow new legs if they lose one. They sometimes also split themselves in two, and start growing new arms to replace the ones that went off with the other half. 25 cm

mouth
This is underneath the centre of the animal. When sea stars eat, they push their stomach out through their mouth and on to their food. Their stomach then digests the food.

99

land snails

Snails, shellfish, octopus and squid are all molluscs. Many molluscs have shells, but not all. Scientists think they are all descended from a common ancestor that had a shell, and that some adapted to living without a shell.

garden snail

The snails we see in our gardens are usually introduced snails. They eat plants. Garden snails are slow movers, taking about a minute to cover just 10 centimetres of pathway.
shell diameter up to 32 mm

eyes on stalks

pūpū giant snail

The bush is home to over 1000 different native snails; some are so tiny they are almost impossible to see, others are giants. The giant snail can live for up to 40 years, if a possum or pig doesn't find it first. This giant snail eats worms. It can be found in the Nelson region. up to 100 mm across

common slug

Slugs are like snails without shells. The common slug that is found in gardens is an introduced species. Slugs eat plants and fungi. Snails and slugs have tongues covered with sharp teeth. up to 3 cm

pūpūharakeke flax snail

Flax snails live in forests in the north of
New Zealand. They eat leaf litter on the
forest floor but can also climb trees.

up to 8.5 cm long

pūpū rangi kauri snail

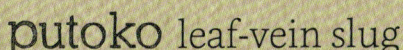

Kauri snails eat worms and other
invertebrates. Like the giant snail and
the flax snail, they are nocturnal. They used to be
found in the kauri forests in the north of New Zealand,
but they are now very rare. Introduced pigs, possums and
rats are a big problem for these snails. They also have fewer
places to live as some of their habitat has been taken
over by people. up to 8 cm

putoko leaf-vein slug

The leaf pattern on these native slugs could be good
camouflage. They eat fungi and algae in the bush.
All snails and slugs need to keep moist. Shells
help keep snails from drying out, and so
does the slime on slugs, but they also
live in damp places. up to 15 cm

sea snails

papatai turret snail

Like snails that live in the garden, some shellfish also have one large foot, which they use to move along. At the beach, you will find empty shells that were once home to living animals. When the animal dies its soft body decays or is eaten, but because the shell is hard it takes much longer for it to get broken down. This is the shell from a turret snail, which lives on the sandy or muddy seafloor. 8 cm

pūpū karikawa
Cook's turban snail

The Cook's turban snail lives on the rocky shore. It grazes on algae and seaweed. 9 cm

ngākihi limpet

Limpets graze on algae and seaweed. They hold on tight to rocks so they are not washed away by the tides and the currents. 5 cm

pūpū rore Arabic volute

The Arabic volute buries itself in sand, using a tube to breathe. At night, it comes out and eats other shellfish such as pipi. 12 cm

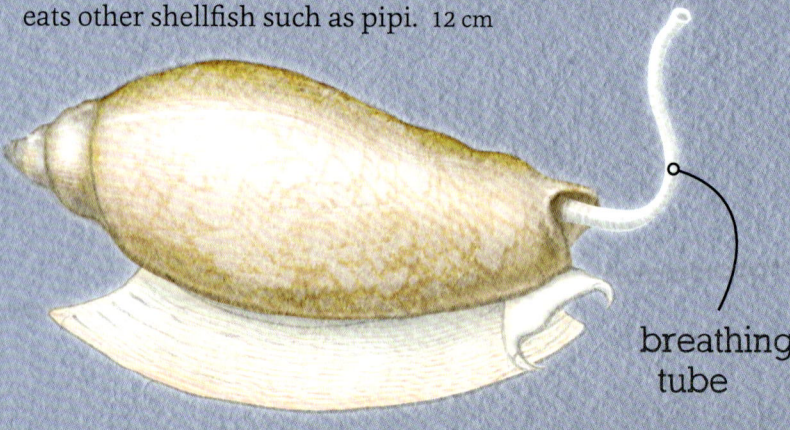

breathing tube

totorere ostrich foot snail

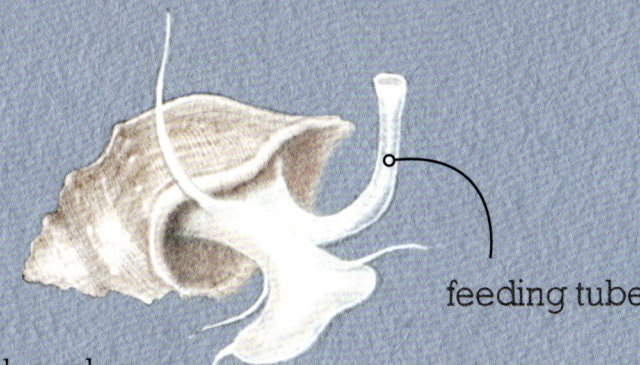

feeding tube

Ostrich foot snails also bury themselves
in sand. They breathe through tubes.
The tubes make the holes that you see
on the beach. 8 cm

breathing holes – shellfish
breathe oxygen, which they can
filter out of seawater

pāua

There are several different species of pāua.
This one is the largest. It has a black foot, which
it uses to move around on the rocks. Pāua live
on rocks up to 10 metres deep. They eat algae and
seaweed. It might seem odd to think of pāua as a
snail, but look closely at its shell and you can
see that although it is a lot flatter than
other snails, it still has a spiral
shape. 16 cm

empty shell – colourful pāua
shell is popular for making jewellery

sea snails

kawari whelk

Whelks eat dying or dead animals and can smell their food from a long distance away. There are at least ten different whelk species; some live on mud flats, others on the rocky shore. 4 cm

ngaeti periwinkle

You will often see periwinkles at the rocky shore on rocks out of the water. They live at the high-tide line, in what is called the 'splash zone'. They eat algae that they find on the rocks. 1 cm

whetiko mud snail

Mud snails live on mud flats where they eat mud! The mud contains bits of food such as algae or seaweed. The mud snail poos out the rest of the mud, leaving a trail of mud waste behind them. 2 cm

pūpū cat's eye snail

Apart from the shell that the animal lives in, cat's eye snails also have a flat round shell like a door or a lid. They close it to protect themselves from predators or from drying out when the tide has gone out. People call this flat piece of shell a cat's eye or kanohi pūpū. 7 cm

freshwater snails & shellfish

freshwater snail

Freshwater snails eat algae. One common freshwater snail is also called the New Zealand mud snail. This snail has become a pest overseas where it has been introduced by mistake.
up to 12 mm

freshwater limpet

Freshwater limpets are tiny. Like marine limpets they live on rocks eating algae. One species of freshwater limpet has slime that glows bright green when they are disturbed. up to 1 cm

kākahi freshwater mussel

Kākahi can be found in lakes or streams where there is soft sand or mud. Like other mussels (page 106) they are filter feeders: they sieve the water for scraps of food. There are fewer kākahi now, as there are fewer suitable places for them to live. up to 9 cm

freshwater clam

Freshwater clams are also called fingernail clams. They are bivalves (page 106). A baby clam lives within its parent's gills until it grows a shell of its own. under 1 cm

shellfish

All the shellfish on these two pages, as well as the freshwater mussel and clam (page 105) are bivalves. Bivalves are shellfish that have two shells joined at a hinge. 'Bi' means 'two'. They open their shells to feed or to move around. The rings on the shells show how old they are. More rings mean the shellfish is older.

hinge

kuku green-lipped mussel

Green-lipped mussels are farmed in the sea in some places around New Zealand. The mussels grow on ropes in the water and are harvested when they are big enough. up to 15 cm

tipa scallop

Scallops live out at sea. They swim by taking in water then squirting it out, which pushes them along. Scallops have one curved shell and one flat shell. 15 cm

tio repe Pacific rock oyster

Rock oysters attach themselves to rocks. Often so many will attach themselves to the same rock that it becomes an oyster reef. The outside of the shell is rough and the inside smooth. 8 cm

toretore blue mussel

All mussels hold on to rocks or other surfaces with tough threads that are near their hinges. They filter the water to catch tiny particles to eat. 12 cm

pipi

Pipi are found in sandbanks. Like many other bivalves they are popular to eat. There are rules around how much shellfish can be gathered to ensure there are enough left to breed. 6 cm

tuangi cockle

Cockles are usually found in mud flats and estuaries. Cockles live just below the surface of the mud. They take in seawater through a feeding tube and filter out food, and they let the seawater out through another tube. Cockles can't live if they get buried by too much sediment or if there is too much pollution. Counting cockles is a good way of finding out about the health of an estuary. 4 cm

tuatua

foot
for burying
into the sand

Tuatua, pipi, cockles and triangle shells bury themselves in the sand or mud. They use their single foot to dig in to the sand. They breathe and feed through tubes. Tuatua are found under sandy beaches. 8 cm

kaikaikaroro triangle shell

These shellfish are surf clams. They live on the sea floor further out from the beach, below the surf. 7 cm

octopus, squid & other molluscs

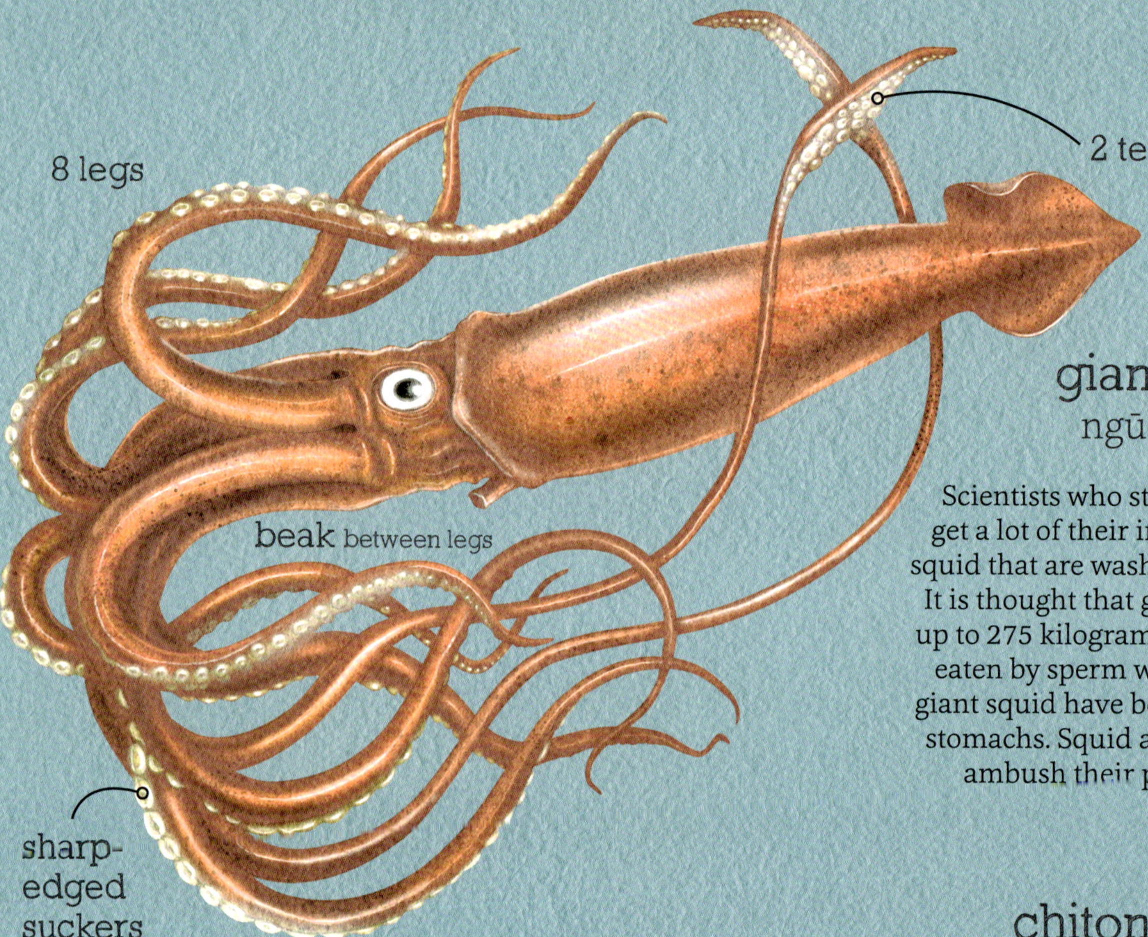

8 legs

2 tentacles

giant squid
ngū

Scientists who study giant squid get a lot of their information from squid that are washed up on beaches. It is thought that giant squid weigh up to 275 kilograms. Giant squid are eaten by sperm whales – beaks of giant squid have been found in their stomachs. Squid are predators that ambush their prey. up to 13 m

beak between legs

sharp-edged suckers

chiton papatua

The parts of chiton shells move separately, which makes it easy for them to bend and squeeze into narrow gaps. Chitons live on the rocky shore. up to 4 cm

ngū arrow squid

Arrow squid live in schools. They are eaten by many sea creatures including birds and whales. They are also one of the most common squid caught for people to eat. up to 40 cm

wheke octopus

The name octopus comes from Greek and means 'eight footed'. Octopuses dig holes in the sea floor, hide in tiny spaces in reefs or build a home out of rocks. If they are threatened, octopuses can squirt out ink to distract predators. Octopuses eat shellfish and crayfish. up to 2 m

pūpū tarakihi
paper nautilus

The female paper nautilus octopus creates a shell to protect its eggs. Empty shells are sometimes found washed up on beaches. up to 20 cm across

ram's horn

Ram's horn shells that you find on the beach are not shellfish at all but come from inside a squid. 2 cm

nudibranch

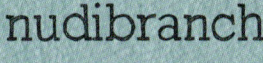

Pronounced 'noo-dee-brank', this clown nudibranch's bright colours are a warning that it is poisonous to eat. Nudibranchs are molluscs that have evolved to live without a shell. They live in rocky reefs and near the rocky shore. There are many different species. up to 6 cm

glossary

algae Similar to plants but without roots or stems. Algae grows on rocks or floats in water

aquatic An animal that lives in water

braided river A river that spreads into channels and criss-crosses stones and gravel

camouflage Colour or shape of an animal that matches its surroundings so that is hard to see

carnivore An animal that eats other animals

declining Getting fewer and fewer in numbers

echolocation Use of echoes to detect and locate prey or other objects

endangered At risk of becoming extinct

herbivore An animal that only eats plants

introduced Animals or plants that are not native to New Zealand and have been brought here by people, either deliberately or by mistake

invertebrates Animals that don't have backbones

larvae Young of insects

leaf litter Fallen leaves and other plant material on the ground

mainland The North and South islands of New Zealand, not Stewart Island or the smaller offshore islands

migrate To move from one area to another at a particular time of year and then back again, usually to feed or breed

moult To get rid of its body covering and grow a new one, like a penguin growing new feathers or a crab growing a new shell

native An animal that is naturally in New Zealand. In this book we use the word native to describe animals that have arrived in New Zealand naturally (for example, birds that flew here and now live here) or animals that are found nowhere else in the world (can also be called 'endemic')

nocturnal An animal that is usually active at night-time

pest An animal or plant that is unwanted or does damage, such as stoats

predator An animal that hunts and eats other animals

sanctuary A place where animals are protected from introduced species

scavenger An animal that eats anything it can find, including animals that are already dead

species A way of describing each different type of animal in a family

threatened At risk of becoming endangered or extinct

venomous An animal that has a poisonous bite or sting

vulnerable At risk of becoming endangered or extinct

find out more

Visit wildlife sanctuaries, nature reserves or marine reserves to see native animals and learn more about them. Check out books from your local library or go to these websites:

www.doc.govt.nz/nature/ Department of Conservation, information on native animals, endangered animals, pest animals, marine mammal sightings

www.nzbirdsonline.org.nz New Zealand Birds Online, information and identification of birds

www.landcareresearch.co.nz Landcare Research, information and identification of insects, spiders and bugs

www.marinelife.ac.nz Marine Life, information about creatures that live in the sea

www.reptiles.org.nz New Zealand Herpetological Society, information on reptiles and frogs

www.maoridictionary.co.nz Te Aka Māori/English dictionary, Māori pronunciation

Information for parents and teachers about this book, including more websites and activities:
www.pottonandburton.co.nz/animals-of-aotearoa

index